Metaphors of Education

Studies in Education ISSN 0458-2101

A series of monographs published by Heinemann Educational Books for the Institute of Education, University of London. Other titles in the series:

Further information about Institute of Education publications may be obtained from the Information Officer, Institute of Education, 20 Bedford Way, London WC1H 0AL; or from Heinemann Educational Books, 22 Bedford Square, London WC1B 3HH.

Studies in Education (new series) 14

Metaphors of Education

William Taylor (editor), David Aspin,
R.K. Elliott, Kenneth Charlton,
Liam Hudson, Denis Lawton,
Gerald Holton, Raymond Wilson

HEINEMANN EDUCATIONAL BOOKS
for the Institute of Education, University of London

Heinemann Educational Books Ltd
22 Bedford Square, London WC1B 3HH

LONDON EDINBURGH MELBOURNE AUCKLAND
HONG KONG SINGAPORE KUALA LUMPUR NEW DELHI
IBADAN NAIROBI JOHANNESBURG
EXETER (NH) KINGSTON PORT OF SPAIN

© Institute of Education, University of London, 1984
First published 1984

British Library Cataloguing in Publication Data

Metaphors of education.—(Studies in education; no. 14)
  I. Taylor, William   II. Series
  370'.1   LB41

  ISBN 0-435-80880-X
  ISBN 0-85473-166-0 Pbk

Printed in Great Britain by Biddles Ltd. Guildford

Contents

Note on Authors

William Taylor is Principal of the University of London. From 1973 to 1983 he was Director of the Institute of Education, University of London.

David Aspin is Dean of Faculty and Professor of Education at King's College, London.

R.K. Elliott is Emeritus Reader in Education in the University of London and a member of the Philosophy of Education Department, Institute of Education, University of London.

Kenneth Charlton is Emeritus Professor of the History of Education in the University of London. From 1972 to 1983 he held the History of Education Chair at King's College, London.

Liam Hudson is Professor and Head of the Department of Psychology, Brunel University.

Denis Lawton is Professor of Education and Director of the Institute of Education, University of London.

Gerald Holton is Mallinckrodt Professor of Physics and Professor of the History of Science, Harvard University.

Raymond Wilson is Professor of Education and Chairman of the School of Education, University of Reading.

Acknowledgements

This book and the series of special lectures from which it arose have been the work of many hands. I should like to thank each of the contributors for being willing to turn their original papers into chapters, and for tolerating the queries of an editor who makes no claim to knowledge of their specialist fields; the students, teachers and colleagues who participated in the lecture series, and who sharpened and clarified some of the issues through subsequent discussion; Dame Mary Warnock and Professor Robert Dearden for their helpful comments on the typescript; Mr Denis Baylis, Information Officer of the Institute of Education, without whose invaluable assistance (and persistence) the book would never have reached print, and who has also prepared the index; and my former secretary, Miss Sue Morrell, who maintained an unflagging interest and commitment to the project from the original planning of the lectures to the typing and retyping of the final manuscript.

We are most grateful to Faber and Faber Publishers for permission to quote six short extracts from *Lord of the Flies* by William Golding; to Mrs Laura Huxley and Chatto and Windus Limited for permission to quote short extracts from *Brave New World* by Aldous Huxley; and to Michael B. Yeats and Macmillan Limited, London, for permission to quote a verse from the W.B. Yeats' poem 'Mad as the Mist and Snow' (*Collected Poems of W.B. Yeats*, Macmillan, London). The verse of W.H. Auden quoted on page 24 is taken from the poem 'As I Walked Out One Evening' (*W.H. Auden: Collected Poems*, Faber and Faber, London).

W.T.
University of London
March, 1984

Introduction
William Taylor

This collection of essays about the use of metaphor in talk and writing about education is based upon the edited scripts of a series of special lectures originally delivered at the University of London Institute of Education.

My own interest in how our choice of metaphors reflects and helps to organize our thinking, talking and writing about educational issues grew out of writing a paper about accountability in education for a Social Science Research Council symposium (Taylor, 1978) and another on a similar theme for a conference of the Australian Council for Educational Administration (Taylor, 1980). It was also stimulated by being asked to speak on the subject of 'quality control' at a conference of the British Educational Administration Society (Taylor, 1981).

In the literature on these topics it was clear that ideas transposed from their original fields of application were being employed to describe, to legitimate and sometimes to explain, complex, multi-determined processes and procedures in ways that, however useful, were often inappropriate to educational contexts. The use of extended metaphors in educational discourse is by no means limited to such contemporary examples. The literature of education abounds with such usages. Education is frequently conceptualized in terms of growth or development. There are references to the mechanics of the learning process. The importance (or the perils) of creativity are stressed. Education is described as a process of initiation, there is an 'education for capability' movement and hardly a minute or a page goes by in talking or writing about education without some more or less active metaphor being invoked.

Interest in metaphor is not limited to any one disciplinary specialism, as will be obvious in the chapters that follow. The first, a shortened version of

1

a lecture I gave to open the series, serves to justify the theme and to indicate some of the ways in which it has been and is being studied. Until a decade ago, when I gave up systematic academic teaching and research in favour of administration, I worked mainly in the sociology of education. Thus the conclusions of this chapter have mainly to do with the part that metaphor plays in setting boundaries to the varieties of educational talk and writing associated with the performance of particular roles.

In the chapter that follows, Professor David Aspin looks at the topic from the viewpoint of a philosopher of education, and relates metaphor to the varieties of linguistic analysis that have been such a strong influence on philosophical writing about education. He also shows the part that metaphor can play in enriching the imaginative grasp of educational concepts and meanings, identifying metaphor as the favourite child of the marriage of memory and imagination.

Another philosopher, R K Elliott, contributes the third chapter and is also concerned with the relationship of metaphor and imagination. Elliott focuses attention on the ubiquitous metaphors of growth and initiation, and concludes that their chief importance lies in their 'rhetorical function, which is to stimulate imagination, to arouse feeling and to prompt action'.

Professor Kenneth Charlton's chapter on the paradox of metaphor shows how many of the root metaphors in use today — horticultural, physical spatial, religious — also found a place in sixteenth-century writing and rhetoric, and discusses the use that was made of metaphor to ease the transition from Latin to vernacular language as the medium of a schooling.

Professor Liam Hudson, in the fifth chapter, relates his own early research progress to attempts to fight his way clear of inappropriate systems of metaphor. His long-standing interest in the role of metaphor in psychological research is applied here not only to his continuing researches, but also to fiction that he has written and to a new book about the image of the body in works of art.

In the next chapter, Professor Denis Lawton narrows the focus to a concern with metaphor in the discussion of curriculum. Cores, spirals, streams, sets and bands are only a few of the more obvious metaphorical usages in this field. He shows some of the limitations of contemporary metaphors, such as curriculum 'objectives' or 'goals', and of curriculum planning based upon such ideas.

The part that metaphor plays in the language of science and of science education is the concern of Professor Gerald Holton, whose analysis ranges widely through classical and contemporary literature, and who rejects the notion that there are distinctions between ordinary and scientific language, that make the use of metaphor legitimate in the one but out of place in the other.

Finally, Professor Raymond Wilson examines the metaphors used in some nineteenth and twentieth-century educational fiction — in Dickens, Eliot, Hardy, Ballantyne, Golding and Huxley. He condemns the tendency to justify a continuing place for the arts and the humanities within the curriculum in terms dictated by the very scientific culture that, in some of its variants, purports to supplant them as the source of our values and the basis of our knowledge.

Although these authors' approaches to the theme of metaphor in talk and writing about education are as diverse as their disciplinary specialisms, they concur in acknowledging the importance of recognizing, understanding and assessing the part that metaphor plays in organizing and enriching discourse about education, and in recognizing the dangers of unexamined and uncritical metaphoric usage. I hope that these essays will throw some valuable light on what we are about when we employ the metaphors of education.

Chapter One
Metaphors of Educational Discourse
William Taylor

I learned at school that metaphor was a figure of speech, one of the ways in which ordinary descriptive language was adorned or made more interesting. The function of language itself was too obvious to require explication. If I had thought about it, I would no doubt have concluded that words were assembled into sentences in order to describe things which could be seen or touched or smelled or heard or felt, or to state ideas which existed in people's heads in the present or in the past. Such an explanation would have seemed perfectly satisfactory. Since I wrote neither poetry nor expressive prose, and since the imperatives of my subjects stressed the importance of greater scientific rigour and of more accurate and invariant use of terms, figures of speech held no particular interest for me. Where a metaphor seemed a useful way to enhance a descriptive statement, or to make a prescription more persuasive, I used it. Such usage was as unreflective as a young child's use of grammatical principles in constructing its first sentences.

At university I began to be disabused of my ignorance. Language, it seemed, was not simply a mode of description, a means of symbolizing and communicating experience and ideas. Language did not simply *reflect* changes in certain underlying realities. Instead, through its classifications, categorizations and codes, it *helped to constitute* these realities, shaping our experience and our judgements about the nature of phenomena, providing not merely the currency of circulation and exchange, but the values symbolized by that currency.

During the Seventies, anyone trying to keep abreast of the intellectual tides and currents that helped to fashion thought could not long remain ignorant of the growing number, importance and widening disciplinary scope of language studies. Within the matrix of forces contributing to a greater language awareness, 'vertical', disciplinary, elements were contributed by philosophers, anthropologists, sociologists and historians. 'Horizontal', cross-disciplinary analyses were offered by structuralists and phenomenologists, who sought to enunciate coherent principles of method that would maintain and respect the continuities that link individual and society, thought and action, culture and human biology, rather than fractionate understanding through disciplinary specialization.

In a changing society, language showed itself to be in a state of constant change. As Richards (1950) and others have emphasized, stable meanings can only come from stable contexts. Specialists in lexicolinguistics and glottochronology study ways in which vocabulary, structure, style and other features of language interact with changes in culture, society and polity. Such interactions have begun to be penetrated and understood through multidisciplinary studies and theories of linguistic and social change. New attention is being given to how the rules and practices of language use serve to promote the possibilities of certain kinds of action and exclude the practicability of others.

In all this, the study of metaphor assumes a central position. Far from being a mere linguistic decoration, metaphor comes to be seen as a ubiquitous feature of our thinking and our discourse, the basis of the conceptual systems by means of which we understand and act within our worlds. Traditional dictionary definitions which regard metaphor as a wholly verbal matter, having to do with the relationship of words rather than what Richards calls the 'intercourse of thought', must be judged too narrow.

The Oxford Dictionary (1933) defines metaphor as 'The figure of speech in which a name or descriptive term is transferred to some object different from, *but analogous to*, that to which it is properly applicable' (my italic). But does not the restriction 'analogous to' entail a circularity? It implies that the nature of the analogy can be stated or paraphrased without reference to the metaphor itself. Surely, the nature of the analogy is defined *by* the metaphor? There is no pre-existing set of analogical rules by means of which the legitimacy or illegitimacy of a metaphor can be determined. Here, I am attracted by Max Black's interaction theory of metaphor, originally stated in his *Models and Metaphors* (1962), and reformulated in a later paper (Black, 1977a) in five propositions.

Black claims that in any metaphorical statement there are two distinct subjects, which he identifies as *primary* (1) and *secondary* (2). The secondary subject (e.g. 'society is a *network*') signals the existence of a system of relationships, which Black now calls the *implicative complex*. The metaphor works by (3) projecting this implicative complex upon the primary subject (society). In making metaphors, a process of selection and emphasis is at work (4), linking the primary subject to particular features of the implicative complex. Finally,

> (5) In the context of a particular metaphorical statement the two subjects 'interact' in the following ways: (i) the presence of the primary subject incites the hearer to select some of the secondary subject's properties; and (ii) invites him to construct a parallel 'implicative complex' that can fit the primary subject; and (iii) reciprocally induces parallel changes in the secondary subject. (Black, 1977a, p. 442)

An approach such as that suggested here invests metaphor with a significance lacking in what have been called the 'substitution' and 'comparison' views of metaphor. It stands firmly against the proposition that any metaphorical statement can be replaced by an equivalent literal meaning, or that there is an imputed literal paraphrase which involves some similarity or analogy, and which thus equates metaphor with simile.

Thus, the position I adopt here is that the goodness, fit, truth, or falsity of a metaphor must be assessed in their own terms, not in those of some literal substitute paraphrase.[1] In the words of Nelson Goodman:

> Metaphorical use of language differs in significant ways from literal use but is no less comprehensible, no more recondite, no less practical, and no more independent of truth and falsity than its literal use. Far from being a mere matter of ornament, it participates fully in the progress of knowledge: in replacing some stale 'natural' kinds with novel and illuminating categories, in contriving facts, in revising theory and in bringing us new worlds . . . Metaphorical truth and falsity are as distinct from — and as opposite to — each other as are literal truth and falsity. (Goodman, 1979, pp. 175–6)

The processes of association involved in the making of metaphors are open to interpretation from a number of different perspectives. Donald Schon (1963) has written of the displacement of *concepts*. Turbayne (1962) draws upon Ryle's notion of the category mistake in proposing a definition of metaphor as the presentation of facts of one sort as if they belong to another — or what he calls 'sort crossing'. A metaphor is only alive when there is realization of duality of meaning. When there is no awareness of such duality, when the metaphor comes to be taken literally, so that schools *do* have an output, that man *is* a mechanism, we are dealing with a dead or hidden metaphor; sort-crossing has become sort-trespassing.

We should, however, be cautious about the traditional distinction between live and dead metaphors. Such a distinction is aligned with a literary 'figure of speech' definition of metaphor, rather than that which I have adopted here. The purposes of many participants in educational discourse are best served if the metaphorical nature of their statements remains hidden, if attention is able to be drawn away from the path down which the sustained use of a particular metaphor is leading. Fortunately, many such metaphors can be restored to consciousness without too much difficulty — a little mouth-to-mouth (or perhaps mouth-to-ear) resuscitation can be highly efficacious.

It is clear that to accept the full implications of metaphor as a 'master trope' (Burke, 1945) erodes to a considerable extent the distinction between metaphor and such other figures as metonymy, synecdoche and catachresis. Indeed, many contemporary students of the subject have abandoned any attempt to arrive at precise definitions. As Hawkes (1972, p. 5) has observed, 'the notion of metaphor itself is shaped at any given time by linguistic and social pressures, as well as by its own history: it has no pristine form'. The philosopher Shibles (1971) claims for metaphor the status of one of the central art-forms of mankind — 'There is an art to making metaphors, seeing the world metaphorically, and living metaphors . . . We are engaged in the art of metaphor when we whistle, or arrange flowers in a vase' (p. 1) — and believes that metaphor ought to be taught as a separate course in universities, as one of the arts rather than a function of them. A recent book on the subject (Lakoff and Johnson, 1980) is entitled *Metaphors We Live By*.

Many of those currently interested in the subject of metaphor, especially in the sustained theory-constitutive metaphors (which Black calls archetypes) that organize our thoughts and sometimes direct our endeavours, are concerned neither with enhancing the beauty of our expressive language, nor with ensuring that our descriptive and analytical discourse should be as far as possible literal and metaphor-free, but with developing greater consciousness of the implications of the languages we employ. In Aristotelian terms the command of language involved an ability to use metaphor, 'happily and effectively'. The contemporary sociological and psychological stress on such command derives from the value attached to awareness of the motives of self and others.

Thus, we are directed away from the part that metaphor plays in the expressive function of language towards seeing it, with Ernst Cassirer (*Language and Myth* 1953), as one of the essential conditions of speech, an understanding of which 'leads us back . . . to the fundamental form of verbal conceiving'. Philosophers and linguists in the post-Romantic period have come to see language as an 'organic, self contained, autonomous, system which divides and classifies experience in its own terms . . . language and experience interact and prove fundamentally implicated with each other to an extent that makes it difficult to consider them as separate entities. A language "creates" reality in its own image.' (Hawkes, 1972, p. 59/60)

Language works by means of transference from one kind of reality to another. It is thus essentially — rather than incidentally, or decoratively or even illegitimately — metaphorical. It matters, then, what transferences we are asked to make and encourage others to make in order to classify and to attach meaning to processes labelled 'educational'. Biological, developmental, social, mechanistic, language-game, cybernetic, political, financial, economic — all these varieties are currently on offer in one form or another. Does it make a difference which we choose?

In the task of making the world of education comprehensible and manageable we pile metaphor on metaphor, ordering and classifying for our own purposes phenomena we have already metaphorized, and often in the process destroying the meaning that these phenomena have acquired for those closest to them. Take, for example, the way in which contemporary educational discourse has become politicized. Words such as 'child-centred', 'unstreamed' and 'creativity' on the one hand, and 'basics', 'core curriculum' and 'excellence' on the other have become the property of left and right respectively, serving to label the political and social affiliations of those who employ them. Even the meaning of apparently straightforward descriptions such as 'integrated science', 'political education', physics and classics is covered over with a thick layer of red or blue.

An unreflective use of metaphor is indeed dangerous. When there is no longer any awareness of duality of meaning, when the process of growth or the machine no longer offer useful aids to reasoning but achieve the status of literal truth, then much is at stake. For at that point we become obsessed by our metaphors, enchanted by their descriptive force, corrupted by their ability to generate ever more complex elaborations, the meanings of which depend absolutely upon relations with earlier speculative forms, rather than resting on any empirical base (Arendt, 1978). In educational, as in other forms of discourse, it is a matter of no little importance that the implications of the metaphors we employ or accept are made explicit, and the ways in which they structure our thought, and even our action, are better understood.

Having elaborated the theme of this volume, let me illustrate it with some brief examples.

In the London Institute of Education's eightieth year, it is perhaps appropriate that my first is taken from a work by the first director, Sir John Adams. In his *The Evolution of Educational Theory* (1912) he says:

> Among the genuine materialists the educator finds himself in very optimistic company. Matters are smoothed out, and many of the distressing complications of the educator's relations with the educand disappear when human nature may be treated on a mechanical basis. A machine may be very complex, no doubt, but there is always the possibility of stopping it, and examining it at our leisure. It is the educand's persistence in going on all the time that is so maddening to the conscientious but hesitating educator. Unless the machine can be stopped, most of its charm for the educator is gone. Oliver Wendell Holmes has a figure that can be used in a very disagreeable way. He has the fatiguing fancy that we are all seventy-year-old clocks, wound at the beginning and ticking off our lives. What could be a more exasperating conception for the educator than to imagine his pupils as seven-year-old clocks that come and sit on his benches and tick away their different stages of development, while he can only sit outside and wonder what is going on within. (Adams, 1912, p. 311)

It will be obvious at once that this quotation is full of metaphor. To conceive of human behaviour and response in terms of mechanism is one of the oldest conceits of our language and thought. Indeed, variants of the idea of mechanism have, as Adams indicates, provided the essential structure for some kinds of educational theory, modern versions of which draw heavily on the language of cybernetics, thermodynamics and computing (Dupuy, 1980).

Let us shift the focus. This is from a recent review by Paul Nash[2] (1981) of Gregory Bateson's (1980) collection *Mind and Nature: a necessary unity.*

> Bateson's theory of Mind is holistic. 'Wholes', for him, are made up of combined interaction of differentiated 'parts'. Mental function is immanent in this interaction. Our greatest need is to become aware of these wholes and to avoid being lost in trivia. Because of our focus on trivia, we are almost always unaware of trends in our changes of state. He cites the quasi-scientific fable that, if you can get a frog to sit quietly in a saucepan of water and then raise the temperature of the water slowly and smoothly so that there is no clear moment when the frog should jump, it will not jump. It will be boiled. Bateson speculates: 'Is the human species changing its own environment with slowly increasing pollution and rotting its mind with slowly deteriorating religion and education in such a saucepan?' (p. 413)[3]

There are lots of questions we might want to ask about Bateson's frog-in-the-saucepan metaphor. Is it anything more than a rather ingeniously-constructed image, useful in pointing out to us a perhaps unrecognized aspect of the hidden dangers of gradualness? Or does it go further than this, and begin to act on our thinking in a way that some students of metaphor call 'theory-constitutive' (Boyd, 1979)? Does the frog-in-the-saucepan metaphor have programmatic research-orienting features, serving to point us in the direction of deeper levels of similarity and analogy? Or is the frog-in-the-saucepan a mere literary flourish?

Whatever the status of this particular metaphor of Bateson's may be, he employs others elsewhere in his work that are more than merely insightful and suggestive. For example, his use of 'toxicity' and 'deprivation'. He argues that, for biological organisms, there is always a quantity which has an optimum value. An excess — whether of calcium, oxygen, vitamins, or of psychotherapy, entertainment, sex or money — produces toxic effects. Obvious enough, to the Greeks as to ourselves, but the sort-crossing that Bateson goes on to propose between biological values and money values offers a striking and perhaps fruitful line of thought.

The expansion in the sheer quantity and scale of dissemination of organized knowledge during the twentieth century and the multiplicity of disciplinary, sub-disciplinary, multi and interdisciplinary groupings, has enormously increased the range of metaphors available for use in educational discourse. As Dupuy (1980) shows, there has been a positive flowering of informational, biological, organizational and other metaphors, most of these being put forward without any epistemological precautions, and not being worth much.

I have tried to show in recent papers on the idea of 'accountability' in education (Taylor 1980) and that of 'quality control' (Taylor, 1981), that many of these metaphors masquerade as models, without any of the care that is needed to separate out the usable from the unusable parts of the metaphor.

In scientific discourse, models have many of the characteristics of metaphor but, if they are to be tenable, must first be pruned of their more dangerous branches. Once the unusable parts have been identified, they must be avoided. It is not even permissible to use them for stylistic purposes. As Mary Midgley (1980) has pointed out, the metaphor of mechanism in biology can only be employed if one is careful to exclude the notion of a mechanism requiring an inventor or a maker. In criticizing the concept of the 'selfish gene', she presses the point that the legitimacy of this metaphor is undermined by retaining that part which seems to attribute a conscious motive. It is only through retaining this unusable branch of the metaphor that the move can be made from 'genes are selfish' to 'people are selfish'.

Midgley's points underline one aspect of metaphorical usage that is nearly always significant, especially so in education where a discourse is prescriptive concerning relations between people. Metaphors can be seductively reductionist, a tendency much in evidence with the rise of ideas about 'accountability', 'quality control', 'common cores' and the like. To take just the first of these, 'accountability' came to education by an indirect route. Its impact cannot be understood by going to the dictionary, which suggests that as an adjective 'accountable' means 'bound to give account, responsible and explicable', and, as a noun, (1) counting and calculation, (2) a reckoning of debit and credit in money or service, (3) an estimation, and finally (4) a narration or report. Although several of these meanings are present in the use that is made of accountability in educational discourse, the term itself serves as a metaphor for a host of meanings from the worlds of business, financial management and government. First used in relation to education at the end of the Sixties (Lessinger and Tyler, 1971), the word soon began to feature commonly in speeches and writings about educational topics. There are now many thousands of articles, monographs and books that contain references to issues of accountability.

'Quality control' is another metaphor that has been much in evidence in educational discourse during recent years. It deserves a little attention. The word 'quality' has no real meaning except in relation to some explicit and agreed, or implied but generally understood, *function*. In the words of a textbook of factory and production management:

> Quality is not a property which has an absolute meaning; a high quality pair of beach shoes can well be a very low quality pair of walking shoes, a low quality billiard cue can be a very high quality pea-stick. The quality of an article has a meaning only when related to *function* ('that . . . which makes it work or sell') and the isolation of function is rarely simple. (Lockyer, 1974, p. 50)

Thus, given that education serves many different functions for different people, the use of the word 'quality' does nothing to resolve long-standing debates about what education should be for, about how benefits and resources should be distributed, whether the imperatives of civilization and of human potentiality are best served by common or diversified curricula.

If quality is to be established in relation to fitness for some purpose, such purposes cannot rationally be defined independent of the means available for their achievement. However idealized or moralized the form in which a purpose first presents itself, by the time it has been legislated for in public policy or become an administrative objective, it has usually been greatly modified to take account of materials and means presently or putatively to hand. The relationship between purpose and possibility is never unidirectional.

When public policy could reflect unarticulated or tolerated distinctions in worth or desert — gold, silver or bronze, an IQ of 130 or one of 90, the deserving or the undeserving poor — it was possible to derive differences in function which legitimated variations in quality of provision. With the dissolution of such distinctions it has become increasingly difficult to justify anything but 'the best'. Variations in expenditure, accepted (not always wisely) as proxies for the level of service provided, are readily subject to scrutiny and criticism.

All this inevitably creates problems in trying to apply quality control concepts to education. In manufacturing, the meaning of quality control is quite narrowly defined. It is 'a term usually used in the U.K. to cover those techniques of inspection based upon sampling methods'. The key factor in any process of quality control is the determination of a specification. Assuming that we are able to determine the specification appropriate to the achievement of a particular purpose or purposes, how do we then go about the business of ensuring that this specification is met?

Determining the acceptable level of variability is an essential element in any specification. One thou less or more, six hundred hours from one electric bulb and 1,800 from another in the same batch, may or may not be acceptable. In any process executed by different people using different machines and different pieces of material there will be, despite every effort of standardization, residual variations which those responsible for quality control regard as inherent to that particular process. In addition, there will be sources of variation that arise from assignable causes — defects in raw material, the mood of the operator (the Friday afternoon car we all dread buying), the type of supervision exercised, and so on. The line between residual and assignable variation is not absolute, and is likely to be determined by economic considerations.

It has been argued that in recent years the customers of education have shown themselves less willing to accept that variations in output are due to residual factors, and would like to tighten the specification to obtain a more accurate identification of the assignable causes of variability. The task of identifying what is residual and what is assignable has not been left to the professionals. The air has been thick with assertions by politicians and public figures, on behalf of parents and taxpayers, concerning the inadequacy of teacher training, the weakness of heads, the fragmentation of curriculum and the lack of proper supervision and inspection. Measures of need and satisfaction are notoriously unreliable. However spurious the recent inflation of discontent, education is certainly not exempt from the greatly heightened sense of expectation that characterizes open societies with high standards of living and high anticipated rates of return from individual investment in additional years of schooling. The language of quality control offers a metaphor for recent changes in public attitudes in the distinctions it offers between high, medium and low cases of what is called 'relative precision'.

High relative precision exists when the specification tolerance — the gap between the lower and upper specification limit — is wider than the current natural tolerance. For example, where the specification demands plus or minus five thous, and the actual distribution of completed items is fully contained within a distribution of plus or minus three thous, high relative precision exists. Medium relative precision relates to where the fit between specification and process tolerance is for one reason or another much tighter. Low relative precision occurs when the process tolerance is wider than the specification range.

Now, in the high relative precision case, the manufacturer is in the happy position of being able to satisfy his customers with very little effort. He could even allow process tolerances to drift up or down a bit without running into trouble. The fact that the performance of some plants was much better than that of others, would not matter too much. There is opportunity to modify materials, methods, levels of supervision and so on without incurring penalty. This is less so in the medium precision case, emphatically not so when low precision is the rule. Then, something has to be done. Customer satisfaction might be maintained by a higher level of final reject, but this is both wasteful and inefficient. The process might be improved so that the residual variability diminishes. The customer might be persuaded to widen the specification, especially if it can be shown that the limits of improvement using existing or likely technologies have already been reached (and provided that someone else is not offering existing or improved specification at a comparable price).

Sticking with the metaphor, we can now say that during the past decade or so the provision of many kinds of educational service, especially those offered during the compulsory years of primary and secondary schooling, has moved from a position of high to one of low relative tolerance. Until fairly recently, the specifications have been loosely drawn. Even when they *have* existed, customers were willing to accept that failures were the result of irreducible residual variability in the educational process, for which educators themselves could not be expected to assume responsibility. At one level, popular mythology invoked silk purses and sows ears and equine responses to confrontations with water, whilst, at another, research findings on the distribution of ability and the effects of different patterns of motivation were quoted in defence.

Not all customers, of course, have identical tastes. Some wanted such esoteric products as greater social equality. Yet confronted with failure to deliver, even they went away more or less peacably when presented with an explanation that suggested they were wrong to have wanted such a thing in the first place, but if they still hankered after it, they would be wise to deal with a group of quite different firms.

It is only in respect of some products that the potential customer provides the specification, invites tenders, chooses the most satisfactory, signs the contract and sits back to await delivery (although the short-lived history of 'performance contracting' in the United States of America showed that some people found even this model attractive). It is quite customary, and not only when the number of potential manufacturers is limited, for a specification to emerge from a lengthy and detailed process of negotiation between customer and manufacturer, in the course of which the desirable and possible become reconciled at a price acceptable to both parties. Quality control then becomes a matter of ensuring that the agreed specification is met, or that in the light of productive experience it is modified by means of further negotiation.

This is a more promising conceptual framework in terms of which to fit discussion of quality control in education than one which implies a market situation in conditions of perfect competition, with the relationship between customer and manufacturer mediated solely by price. In the real world the education system is also the consumer of many of its own products, and many of the customers are themselves involved in some aspect of the production process. Information exchange in the course of negotiation between interlocking networks of national and local politicians, administrators, representatives of teachers' organizations, members of subject associations, interest groups and so forth, not only in formal settings but through contacts at conferences, in the columns of the educational press, at drinks parties, even in the street, constitute a continuous process by means of which agreements and understandings emerge as to what constitute reasonable and realistic expectations for the 'output of particular parts of the system'. Specifications, in other words, are negotiated, not simply put out to tender.

It will be clear that an interpretation of quality control drawn from industrial practice (those techniques of inspection based upon sampling methods) is of only very limited application to the determination of quality in non-marketed goods such as 'education'. There are problems in defining quality. The use of the word 'control' implies a pattern of relationships that bears little relationship to the human reality of institutional and systems management. The production metaphor suggests a degree of precision in the process of inspection that we know cannot be achieved in educational settings. I have indicated elsewhere (Taylor, 1981) that there are risks in using the metaphor of quality control to package that great variety of processes — validating, accrediting, credentialling, testing, monitoring, inspecting, advising — which might usefully contribute to the quality of education. Especially so, when such processes depend not upon the degree of control that one person or agency exercises over other people or agencies, but on mutual understanding, on the negotiating of agreements, the provision and exchange of information, and above all on the personal commitments that individuals make to the improvements of their practice. The images invoked by quality control invite unhelpful comparisons with processes that have little to do with education, and lend a superficial technological glamour to bureaucratic values. The language that such images encourage us to use erodes and discredits the human elements of mutuality, trust, reciprocity, sympathy, dependence, scepticism, understanding, responsibility and commitment, that in various mixes characterize the complex relations of parents, teachers, heads, advisers, inspectors and education officers.

The economist Joan Robinson has this to say about certain of the models in use in her own field:

> Mathematical operations are performed upon entities that cannot be defined; calculations are made in terms of units that cannot be measured; accounting identities are mistaken for causal laws; differences are identified with changes; and one-way movements in time are treated like movements to and fro in space. The complexity of models is elaborated merely for display, far and away beyond the possibility of application to reality. (Robinson, 1979, p. 21)

It is useful to remind ourselves that it is not only educationists who are guilty of metaphorical elaboration. And has it not been said, with reference to the burgeoning literature about the origins of man — a literature divided by the competing metaphors of humans as co-operators and humans as aggressive predators — that the actual evidence on which the whole discourse is based could be assembled without difficulty into one small room, leaving plenty of space for at least one sociobiologist, one eugenicist, one cultural anthropologist and one Marxist to argue it out to a conclusion, or perhaps even to find some basis of common understanding?

Metaphors evoke relationships — in Black's terms, between the primary and secondary subject, in those of Richards, between tenor and vehicle. The making of the relationships between primary and secondary subject, between tenor and vehicle, is very much a task for the hearer or the reader. Interpretation involves the filling in of connections. The trying out of such connections which, as Empson (1930) argues, is the essential feature of the potential use of language, constitutes experimentation that is by no means random. Indeed, since language itself is a social institution, so are the tactics of establishing connectiveness social. The relations established between primary and secondary subject, between tenor and vehicle, are social relations.

To make extensive use of metaphor with the expectation of being understood, involves assumptions about the characteristics and membership of a linguistic community, the rules of which will set limits on the degree of ambiguity that is inherent in *any* metaphor. The 'appropriate' interpretation of metaphor requires inside knowledge.

An example is provided by Williams' (1980) work on *Figures of Thought in Roman Poetry*. Williams contends that for the poet to say one thing with the expectation that his reader would understand that he meant quite another, several relationships between the two meanings being possible, was dependent upon a particular view of the nature and function of poetry characteristic of the period 60–65 BC to the death of Horace. To disentangle the poet's meanings required the judgement and privileged information available only to a group of 'insiders'. It also demanded time. It was thus opposed to traditional rhetorical modes, reliant as they were on the direct perception of meaning. Williams stresses that the ability of readers to cope with the metaphoric styles used by, for example, Catullus and Horace, presupposed similarities of 'education, social position and sympathetic understanding'.

Cohen, T. (1979), has argued that metaphor is one means for what he calls the 'achievement of intimacy', serving to draw together the maker and the appreciator of a metaphor. In the process of recognizing that something has a metaphorical meaning, and in trying to make out what that meaning is, '. . . the hearer typically employs a number of assumptions about the speaker: what the speaker believes, what the speaker believes about what the hearer believes (which includes beliefs about what the speaker thinks the hearer can be expected to believe about the speaker)'. In tracing changes that have taken place in metaphorical usage over time, Hawkes (1972) has shown how in the sixteenth, seventeenth and most of the eighteenth centuries, metaphors performed a didactic function, manifesting truths, ideas and values that would carry public assent, reinforcing, rather than challenging or questioning, established views of the world.

The metaphors of education represent the claims made by groups to impose their own sets of meanings on experience. Metaphor is part of a linguistic code that helps to create relevance and to constrain social identities. Educational discourse is conducted in accordance with codes associated with certain role performances — for example those of educational psychologists, sociologists, philosophers and historians; school, college and university administrators; teachers and headmasters; inspectors, curriculum consultants and others involved in educational activities. These codes embrace a variety of metaphorical usages, some of which are common, many of which are particular to a group of 'insiders', who share a set of agreed references.

The particular *content* of the set of relationships between primary and secondary subject, tenor and vehicle, that Black identifies as the *implicative complex*, are the product of what Steiner (1972) has called the resonance effect, by means of which both 'text and the reader's response are organized by firm habits of schooled recognition . . .' Steiner has much that is important to say about the undeclared social and psychological presumptions that underlie any corpus of agreed reference, and which facilitate the economy of statement that makes possible a literary style. Such a style, such a shared referential literacy, is inevitably associated with the drawing of boundaries, with definitions of membership that are inherently exclusive as well as inclusive — élitist if you like — just as much in the case of Marxist intellectuals as for administrative mandarins. As Frank Kermode has put it in another context:

> The real difference between the outside and the inside is marked by the insistence of the outsider that he can say what he likes about Shakespeare and the tacit knowledge of the institution, which he therefore hates, that nothing he says is worth attending to. (Kermode, 1977, p. 164)

Within many of the groups that participate in educational discourse there are distinctive codes and patterns of metaphorical usage which in creating a shared referential literacy also serve to mark off boundaries and define conditions of membership. In any discourse that draws concepts and theories from a variety of disciplines in an effort to enhance understanding of and control over a practical activity such as teaching, there is enhanced scope for metaphoric formulation and utterance, and a danger that metaphors, torn from the disciplinary context which gives them a more or less settled meaning, will get out of control (permitting what in Saussurian terms might be called the autonomy of the signifier), eliding or ignoring variations in the meaning of words taken from different disciplinary codes. With a discourse based upon the organized study of a subject matter that does not have distinctive truth criteria, that lacks distinguishable public traditions of enquiry, and which is not rooted in a recognizable form of knowledge, there are obvious risks that the elaboration of metaphor for the purposes of boundary definition will become more significant than its use for the purpose of increasing understanding

All this will tend to increase the proportion of abstract terms within the discourse, providing a currency that may be of great importance in strengthening role identification for insiders, but which renders such discourse increasingly opaque to those who are not members of the particular group. In terms that have been made familiar by Basil Bernstein, the form of the social relations among professional educators generates distinctive linguistic codes which serve to transmit the culture of the group, to constrain the behaviour of its members, to determine the conditions that will govern identification as a member of the group, and to shape habitual modes of thought.

The recent stress upon classroom research represents a recognition of the weaknesses of forms of educational discourse built upon metaphorical world images (Weber), 'world hypotheses' (Pepper), archetypes (Black), or root-metaphors (MacRae), that have very little to do with the relations of a teacher and a student in a classroom or a school. Such metaphors are principally concerned with asserting what education does ('education as social engineering'), or legitimating a particular set of educational principles ('education as initiation') or proposing theory-constitutive analogies ('education as information processing'). The elaboration of particular root-metaphors, such as biological and botanical notions of growth and development, into more or less fully developed educational theories, suggests a tacit pedagogy that may take little account of what is physically and socially possible in buildings called schools, divided up into separate classes staffed on a ratio of one to eighteen or more, and subject to stringent resource constraints.

Here architecture can offer a useful metaphor for education. Geoffrey Scott (1914) defined architecture as 'the art of organizing a mob of craftsmen'. The development of mass education in the nineteenth century produced a rash of works concerned with the art of organizing a mob of teachers. When educational discourse loses touch with that task, it suffers the fate of an architecture that takes insufficient account of what at a given time is possible in terms of organization and technique. In Scott's words:

> You can pass, in poetry, at a leap from Pope to Blake, for the sleepiest printer can set up the most original remarks. But the conceptions of an architect must be worked out by other hands and other minds than his own. Consequently, the changes of style in architecture must keep pace with the technical progress of the crafts. And if, at the bidding of a romantic fashion, an abrupt change of style be attempted, then the technique and organization required by the new ideal must not be more exacting than those employed by the existent art. For neither technique nor organization can be called into being suddenly and at will. (Scott, 1914, p. 41)

The individualized nurture implied by growth and development theories failed to take account of the difficulties that fallible and often inexperienced teachers would face in trying to establish and maintain some kind of social and cognitive order among thirty-five children with very varied levels of motivation and achievement, in often less than ideal physical conditions, with only limited teaching resources and very few sanctions in the case of non co-operation. The failure of individualization so conceived is apparent in recent reports from H.M. Inspectorate, in research findings such as those of Brian Simon's *ORACLE* project, and in numerous studies from the United States, reasserting the benefits, in terms of learning outcomes, of a more teacher-centred, didactic, structured approach to classroom practice. (See Medley, 1979; Rosenshine, 1979; and for a critique of such findings, McNamara, 1981)

In human affairs, to look for the one true meaning of a word is not only chimerical, it is also potentially repressive. Ambiguity is not simply a weakness. Empson (1930) in his *Seven Types of Ambiguity* states that he will use the term 'in an extended sense, and shall think relevant to my subject any verbal nuance, however slight, which gives room for alternative reactions to the same piece of language'. The possibility of such 'alternative reactions' is an important key to the kinds of relationships that should properly characterize educational settings — whether those of the infant classroom or the research laboratory (Knorr, 1980). The presence of ambiguity leaves room for the possibilities of *negotiation*, which is the essential condition for the establishment of legitimacy (Ackermann, 1980). In language, as in politics, balancing the claims of individual and society requires a mixed economy of publicly owned and certified meanings on the one hand, and a more or less free market of ambiguous, contested, metaphorical expression on the other, each system — the scientific and consensual as well as the rhetorical and programmatic — being open to influence from the other.

The purveyors of 'accountability', 'quality control', 'child centredness', 'equality of outcome', 'the basics' and the other current metaphors must compete for our custom in the market-place of ideas and policies. The process of negotiation made possible by the metaphorical and ambiguous nature of the language in which their offerings are couched is not a distracting and ultimately perhaps unnecessary waste of time; it is the very stuff of what it means for the individual to experience a sense of freedom in a world where the only ultimate certainty is his or her own extinction.

Since this chapter is intended to provide a beginning, it would be wrong to offer a conclusion. I have sought to make clear that metaphor is not just the business of the poet or the literary critic, but represents one of the ways in which many kinds of discourse — including discourse about education — are ordered and structured, a central feature of the production and reproduction of meaning. The purpose and outcome of a great deal of what is said and written about education, however 'scientific' its form, is to persuade and convince. It seeks to establish a basis for agreement on what is, and on what should be done. Metaphor is an essential element in such a discourse. In the words of W.V. Quine:

> It is a mistake, then, to think of linguistic usage as literalistic in its main body and metaphorical in its trimming. Metaphor, or something like it, governs both the growth of language and our acquisition of it. What comes as a subsequent refinement is rather cognitive discourse itself, at its most drily literal. The neatly worked inner stretches of science are an open space in the tropical jungle, created by clearing tropes away. (Quine, 1979, p. 160)

Educational discourse is for the most part still a trop(e)ical jungle. But is the contrast between jungle and clearing really as sharp as this? This is a question for philosophers to answer. Professor David Aspin addresses this and other issues in the next chapter.

Notes

1. For a contrary view and discussion of this issue, see Donald Davidson, 'What metaphors mean', and Max Black, 'How metaphors work: a reply to Donald Davidson', both in Sacks (1979).
2. Paul Nash was in the chair on the occasion of this lecture's first delivery.
3. Bateson's work is, of course, rich in such metaphor, and he has a good deal to say about its use (Bateson, 1973, especially p. 174 ff.).

Chapter Two
Metaphor and Meaning in Educational Discourse
David Aspin

The chief football reporter of *The Times* recently recounted how he had approached a certain team's manager with a query about his forays into the transfer market over the summer. 'Oh, I've got a few irons in the fire', the manager is said to have replied, 'but I'm holding them close to my chest'. A similar solecism was attributed to the Rev Dr Peter Marshall, who was chaplain to the Senate of the United States. Before the start of a session one day he was reported to have prayed that the Lord 'should open up the windows of our souls and let in Thy pure light to recharge our batteries'. And lately a well-known politician wanted to 'break the mould of traditional politics, put a new weapon into the hands of the electorate, and get down to brass tacks at the grass roots of politics'.

Such mixtures of metaphor are apt to raise a smile because they seem to redouble a feature of metaphorical talk that some would regard as its profoundest error: the transference of the logic of one form of discourse to that of another, illegitimately. Such infelicities as the above are derided because they reduplicate the 'category mistake' (Ryle, 1949, pp. 16 ff, 77–9) of which, as some would view it, a metaphor is already a prime example. And behind such a judgement there often lurks the charge that usage of any expression involving metaphor commits one of the cardinal errors of logic — that of fallacy of analogy. It is for this reason that I believe that the investigation of the role of metaphor in educational discourse to be a matter of considerable importance for, as we are all perhaps uncomfortably aware, educational discourse in any milieu, be it school, college, university or school board office, is replete with metaphors of all kinds — sometimes so much so that one cannot see the real problems, topics and issues lying at the heart of the discussion or enquiry for the problems of intelligibility and validity generated by the metaphors that form such a

21

major part of the contributions of the participants. From the time of Plato, whose Myth of the Sun and the Cave in Book VII of *The Republic*[1] was one of the earliest and most elaborate metaphors for the process of being educated aright: to Froebel whose notion of the child as a tender plant growing in a garden added a new term to the German language that has since become international; to the authors of the Plowden Report who coined the aphorism that 'At the heart of every educational process lies the child' (*Children and their Primary Schools*, chapter 2, para. 9) there has been no shortage of example for those who wished to enquire into the question of the meaning and value of such talk in education.

It was hardly to be expected that the frequency and pervasiveness of this phenomenon in educational discourse would go long unremarked. Animadversions on this very topic might almost be said to have gone hand in hand with the rise of the 'new' philosophy of education; certainly C.D. Hardie (1942), D.J. O'Connor (1957) and Israel Scheffler (1960) did as much as they could to alert us to what they saw as the dangers and illegitimacy of this kind of talk. The ideas expressed in it, we were warned by R.F. Dearden, function 'as a symbolic image, pregnant with meaning and rich in emotional appeal' (Dearden, 1968, p. 25; cf. also Komisar, 1961, pp. 24–42). Such features of metaphors as these, of course, led inevitably to their being adopted as the mottoes or titles that serve to define particular educational movements: 'education according to nature', 'education as "Growth" ', 'education as initiation' were all initially metaphors that rapidly acquired the status of symbols to rally the committed or to belabour the heterodox — they became educational slogans, about which, as Komisar (1961) remarked, the only thing we can be clear is that they are quite empty of all positive content. But such has been the power and influence of metaphors of this kind that they have now, to all intents and purposes, become 'dead': they have actually become adopted as the 'standard' terms, assertable in and open to employment in any form of educational discussion.

The trouble with slogans, of course, is that they can mean all things to all men; and there is certainly a systematic vagueness and ambiguity about metaphors that goes some way towards emptying them of all positive content. Of the use made of metaphorical expressions by such 'great educators' as Pestalozzi, Froebel and Herbart, O'Connor tartly remarked:

> Some of them were acute and systematic but mistaken . . . Some were unsubstantiated conjectures . . . Some . . . were unintelligible adaptations of metaphysical concepts. Many of such theorists indeed seem to have taken to heart the rule of method by which Rousseau attempted to explain the nature of

man: 'Let us then begin by laying facts aside, as they do not affect the position'. (O'Connor, 1957, p. 109)

Thus at least one of the causes of the implausibility of any claim for the works of such authors to acceptable academic status as 'theories' (in the strict sense defined by O'Connor and others of his persuasion) was held to reside in the omnipresence and multivocality of the metaphorical expressions making up so much of what passed for educational 'theory'. Small wonder that many of those concerned to elucidate the nature of 'theory' in education and to justify its claim to serious investigation held the view that metaphor ought to be eradicated completely from all critical and rigorous educational discourse. Entwistle put it this way:

> It is arguable that our educational theories would become sharper instruments, less liable to fallacy, if we could dispense with metaphors altogether. (Entwistle, 1970, p. 156.)

And with this view many would have concurred at more recent periods in the growth and development of the disciplined activity of analysing educational talk and trying to render it intelligible that we call philosophy of education. For such a view was symptomatic of a view of metaphor and meaning that long held currency in certain quarters of philosophy proper.

According to this view (which I shall call the 'purist' thesis) metaphor was in some way a 'blot on the escutcheon' of pure and clear communication of meanings between language users. Such philosophers as Stebbing (1942) held that metaphor was simply a confusing or emotive use of language and, when not actually meaningless, quite unsuited to the rigours of scientific or philosophical discourse. For these people a philosophy from which all metaphor had not been purged was in some way logically degenerate; the technical terms of science and philosophy were a distillation of the pristine clarity and simplicity of the ways in which language users sought to transmit ideas to each other without ambiguity or equivocation of any kind. The prime task of any proper science or philosophy was therefore to root out and exclude such uses of language as did not conform to the 'clarity' criterion; and amongst these one of the chief candidates for eradication was metaphor. The implications of this for education were obvious: metaphor was a bar to clear communication in thinking, speaking and writing; though it could be studied as an interesting linguistic phenomenon (along with its variants metonymy, synecdoche and catechresis), the aim of most language teaching based on the 'purist' view was to avoid metaphor if at all possible.

It is clear that the 'purist' view of metaphor and its place in communication is a function of particular metalinguistic preconceptions and chief among these is adherence to a particular theory of meaning. The theory of meaning operating behind such a view will, I suppose, resemble that account of meaning that derives from the Logical Positivists and the Vienna Circle — the claim that all meaningful utterance is restricted to the analytic, such as the tautologies of logic and mathematics, and the empirical, in which propositions may be verified by the evidence of the senses (Ayer, 1946). Talk of an ethical or aesthetic kind is, on this criterion, meaningless and serves only either as an expression of the utterer's *pro* or *con* attitude to the object in question or as a means of promoting, eliciting or establishing the same or a different attitude in the hearer (cf. Stevenson, 1944). Talk of a metaphysical or religious kind is to be dismissed as literally non-sense; and on this basis all transcendental or speculative utterance is to be abandoned or ignored.

While this theory had considerable power and influence in its time and certainly had the merit of ridding philosophy of many of the excrescences that had laughably been called 'philosophy', it put forward, as a criterion of what John Dewey would have called 'warranted assertability' (Dewey, 1938, p. 134) in language, a principle that was both too hard and in any case incoherent. It was too hard because, on this analysis, whole realms of communication and intersubjective understanding that people had found both profoundly meaningful and worthwhile engaging in were suddenly to be ruled out of court. One has only to think, for instance, of the Song of Solomon, Shakespeare's *Tempest*, or to glance at the poem of W.H. Auden 'As I Walked Out One Evening' (November 1937), cited by Bernard Harrison:

> The glacier knocks in the cupboard,
> The desert sighs in the bed,
> And the crack in the tea-cup opens
> A lane to the land of the dead. (Harrison, 1979, pp. 13–14)

to realize that people do say things to each other of a tremendous profundity, complexity, richness and grandeur that simply cannot be comprehended within the philosophy of the verification principle — even if it were itself logically sound, which it is not. The principle of the Positivists, being neither analytic nor empirically verifiable, cannot stand its own test and therefore must fall. And, on the same basis, so too must the 'purist' view of metaphor.

This leaves us with the task of giving some convincing account of the nature and function of metaphor in our ordinary language, as well, of course, as in the worlds of poetry and literature, where it seems especially to be 'at home'. Clearly, if metaphor *is* such an ineradicable 'figure of speech', its ubiquity, power and meaning have in some way to be explained — a problem that, as Alston remarks, has been one of the chief concerns of recent philosophers of language (Alston, 1964, p. 8). Clearly, too, in considerations of the role that metaphor plays in extending language, the philosophy of education, with its abiding interest in the interrelationship of language, thought and culture, has a part to play.

The account of metaphor that has been widely adopted — from the time of Aristotle to that of Max Black (1962) — is that which is enshrined in the commonly held view that there subsists a distinction between the literal and the figurative in the structure of language itself. This view (which I shall call the 'traditional') has something in common with the 'purist' view, for it has similar ontological underpinnings (e.g. that there are real categories in existence), but it is in many respects different from it. For here the use of metaphor is admitted and explained on the basis of there being, allegedly, a 'real' or a 'central' use of terms and then, in addition to this, an 'extended' or a 'parasitic' use of them, in which perhaps some of the central use's properties are lacking or other and different ones are present. This is the way, for instance, some philosopher of education might explain such expressions as 'It's a real education to walk round Soho at night' or 'Muhammed Ali is soaking up a good deal of punishment now', where, it is thought, such utterances are only intelligible in the light of our knowledge of the *real* meanings of education and of punishment.

On this basis metaphor is to be understood or explained as some sort of semantic *extension* or *transference*, that can in some way function for or stand instead of literal sense, and maybe in some respects show us how a familiar object can be seen in a new light. But the main point is that metaphors are only intelligible in so far as they can in some way be paraphrased and the ability to give such a paraphrase depends crucially upon one's prior familiarity with the 'proper', 'central', 'real' or 'literal' meaning of the terms involved.

Clearly there is an underlying theory of linguistic meaning at work here too, and it is not far to seek. It is that all words have some single, basic and essential meaning, which in some way lies at the centre of all possible uses of a word in any circumstances whatsoever and by reference to which the intelligibility of non-standard uses of that term can be assessed. All that we need to be able to get at this central core is a good enough brain, education and ears, or a resident tame philosopher, who, equipped with the sharp-cutting tools of conceptual analysis, will be able to assemble for us a corpus of 'standard' and 'deviant' uses and from these deduce the 'correct' use and the 'paradigm' case, which will then be the touchstone to which all standard uses, such as metaphor, can be referred. And it is only by knowing the 'real' or 'essential' meanings that we shall be able to understand and respond to metaphor and not run the risk of falling into misunderstanding or logical error.

It is, of course, a commonplace amongst logicians that the antiquity of an idea is no guarantee of its rightness and so it is in this case. There are logical objections to the traditional view of metaphor that are fatally debilitating to it. For one thing, it ignores or flies in the face of the facts of the dynamism of language: what *may* have been a standard case or a correct use fifty or even five years ago we have no reason to suppose will continue to be so five or fifty years hence. It also ignores the geographical nature of language: there is no reason to suppose that what is regarded as 'correct' use in Boar's Hill or Brighton will have the same currency in Boston, Mass. or Brisbane. And from this consideration comes a further telling criticism: the 'essentialist' view of meaning is implicitly normative for, instead of seeking to describe language uses in all their multiplicity and heterogeneity, it seeks instead to lay down prescriptions as to how language ought to be used (cf. Edel, 1973). Unfortunately, it just does not follow that what one group of lexicographers or linguistic analysts happen to regard as 'correct' has to be coercive on the rest of us.

This criticism must be added to the point — by now well-established as a result of the work of Waismann (1965), the later Wittgenstein (1953), Austin (1962) and Searle (1969) — that there *are* no 'standard', 'real', 'correct' or 'essential' meanings of terms. To think that there are and to try to find them is to commit oneself to a search for a chimera. D.M. Taylor sums up this objection well:

> Knowing the meaning of a word is not knowing about something which could be presented or described verbally, a definition or an essence: it is not knowing about a thing of any kind. Knowing how to use a word like knowing how to cast a fly is not knowing about some special kind of object. Like knowing how to play tennis or swim, it is a skill. (Taylor, D.M., 1970, p. 165)

This rejection of essentialism has, of course, consequences for the 'traditional' view of metaphor; for if it is not possible to elicit a *real* meaning or to characterize the central or literal uses, then it makes no sense to talk of non-standard, parasitic, deviant, or extended or transferred uses. Thus the 'traditional' view must fall also.

Why this is has to do with the points I made above concerning the dynamism yet restrictedness of linguistic change. The alterations in the significance of the terms 'presently' and 'prevent' since the time of Shakespeare bear this out, as do the very objects about which we use words (what we now call a cupboard was once called a 'press') and the growing diversification of our interests (what Aristotle once thought a sub-domain of philosophy has now been divided amongst empirical, social and philosophical psychologists and psychometricians); while the fact that we use one word about different objects is no guarantee of any underlying connection between them, as Wittgenstein's point about 'games'[3] makes clear. To think that there *must* be something other than accident that connects 'currying chicken' with 'currying favour' and 'currying horses' is to fall into the fallacy of 'essentialism'. Rather it seems that the only safe way here is to adopt the dictum that,

> For a large class of cases — though not for all . . . the meaning of a word is its use in the language.[4]

In other words, there is a theory of meaning that gets over the problems that have to be faced by verificationist, mentalist, causal and other accounts of linguistic meaning: it is to be found, though not without the necessity for some modifications and addition, in the aphorism 'Don't ask for the meaning, ask for the use' (Wisdom, 1952, p. 258).

This doesn't, of course, mean a humpty-dumpty situation in our use of language;[5] we cannot use words exactly as we like. Language is not idiosyncratic; if it were it would cease to be language. The stability and controllability of language lies in its inter-subjectivity, in our 'agreements in judgement' as to our communication and understanding of meaning. Some of these agreements are uncontroversial and long-lasting — 'chair', 'table', and 'door' for instance. Others, however, such as 'art', 'religion', and 'democracy', are much more protean; they are what Waismann (1965) called 'open-textured'.[6] We can only be reasonably clear about what is being intimated by the use of such expressions by paying careful attention to such matters of nuance, pitch and stress in their utterance as may enable us to infer something of the speaker's intentions; by noting the circumstances in which it is said (Wittgenstein, 1953, para. 583); or by engaging in dialogue with the speaker, so that, by a process of interpretation or negotiation, we can establish our own agreements as to meaning and significance for the purposes we have in mind and in the particular institutional contexts in which we operate. For only in this way shall we be able to reduce the ambiguity and multivocality of such 'essentially contested' terms as 'metaphor' and 'education' to some sort of intelligibility and common coinage between participants in a particular area of discourse (Gallie, 1955 and 1956).

This account of 'meaning as use' allows words to carry their character on their faces, so to speak; we see the meaning of terms in the actual occasion of their employment. This means that we have to amplify the above account by considerations deriving from 'speech act' theory and from the notion of intentionality of a speaker's utterance.[7] Once given this, however, we are in a position to give some account of the role and function of metaphor in ordinary language — though it will, I fear, be one that marks a radical departure from the 'purist' and the 'traditional' views. For, if it is the case that words mean what they are 'seen as' meaning, by hearers noting the particular circumstances in which they are uttered and the declared or implicit intentions of the speaker, then the distinction made between 'literal' and 'figurative', 'basic' and 'transferred', 'essential' and 'extended' uses will collapse — and with that, strange though it may seem, between 'real' and 'metaphorical' meanings. As D.M. Taylor puts it:

> From the point of view of the theory of meaning, then, no clear distinction can be drawn between metaphorical and non-metaphorical uses of words. (Taylor, D.M., 1970, p. 170; cf. ibid. p. 168)

Instead, we might want to explain that linguistic phenomenon that is called metaphor as simply another *façon de parler*, as Austin called it, and remark that 'metaphors' are simply words used normally in unusual surroundings, or vice versa, without any expectation that that particular employment of the term will become common, though, as Taylor notes, what all too often happens is that metaphorical usage commonly becomes standard usage, and this occurrence is a part of the normal development of language. For metaphors such as 'education as initiation' and 'the core curriculum' gain currency in proportion as they encapsulate and present particular conceptions, of which the participants in educational discourse had previously an ill-formed awareness only, in a form of such innovation and attractiveness that their appropriateness is immediately judged by all to be beyond question. In this way ideas such as these enter the standard vocabulary of a form of discourse and serve as 'terms of art' within it, in spite of the continued ambiguity in the meaning of such metaphors that patient analysis and a less-ready or enthusiastic acceptance will steadily show. Wittgenstein's well-known example of the 'Duck-Rabbit' (Wittgenstein, 1953, p. 194 ff.) will serve as an example of the ambiguity of this kind of language; indeed much of it *is* what we should ordinarily call 'metaphorical', where in fact all we are doing is daring to risk the 'bewitchment of our intelligence' by calling attention to a feature of our language that is all-pervasive. Indeed, there have been some who have suggested (though wrongly, as I think) that the whole of our language is a metaphor, a series of complicated and elaborate analogies, extensions and transferences by which the infinite can be reduced to the finite, the unknown hooked on to the known. In contradiction to those who have urged that our technical and professional language should be purged of metaphor, others maintain that metaphorical expressions are ineradicably rooted in language itself — without going so far as the cynical assertion of Nietzsche that the concept of truth itself comes from 'a list of worn-out metaphors that have lost their power to affect our senses'.

The thesis here advanced, then, is not dissimilar from, though not perhaps as strong as the thesis of Davidson (1978), that 'metaphors mean what the words, in their most literal interpretation, mean, and nothing more'. For words mean what they are *used to* mean and what they are *seen as* meaning — and some of these uses and meanings are plastic and plurivocal. Not only has the whole of this paper been, from the beginning, permeated by metaphor, metonymy and catachresis; so is the whole of any of our conversations. It is only when we start to take a conscious interest in metaphor that we become aware of the ubiquity of the phenomenon in our language. But I wish now to go further and suggest that this ubiquity is endemic and ineradicable: 'metaphor' is a basic feature of language and we strive in vain to avoid it. No metaphor, no language, is my suggestion.

As good an illustration as any of the centrality of metaphor in any form of discourse is provided by philosophy itself. We remember the terms employed by the Pre-Socratics, taken from nature, navigation, textile manufacture and the construction of musical instruments, in which they attempted to intimate what they saw as the truths of cosmology and ontology; we may recall such statements as Hegel's, 'The Spirit possesses God in proportion as it partakes in the Absolute'; and we note the preoccupations of some modern logicians with such notions as purity, rigour, clarity and comprehensibility and note the way they employ the languages of space, time, grasping, transport and structure. It is easy then to draw the conclusion that even philosophy is permeated with metaphor, without knowing it. Indeed it has been argued by Pepper (1948) that philosophical development has come from seven or eight basic metaphors (formalism, mechanism, contextualism, etc.), such that a small number of root metaphors has provided the evidential source of the categories of any philosophical system. But these metaphors also provide a second level of abstract structures, which have their own cognitive power and fruitfulness for generating further and more complex explanations of the world. Metaphor, he maintains, is productive of conceptual thinking, which can then be judged on its fertility and explanatory power.

This has to do, I believe, with the most fundamental matters of being and perception. The Pre-Socratics were preoccupied with the problem of the One and the Many: with the fact that our most basic contact with the world of phenomena shows it to be hugely complex and highly heterogeneous. The plurality of our sense impressions we try to organize and render intelligible by picking them out by means of diverse terms and categorizing according to some sort of scheme. The problem is, of course, from where do we get these terms, that form the basis of our categorizations; it is not enough to say, with Heidegger (1971), that 'language is a gift that opens the world to us and it is impossible for us to conceive of it from the outside of that'. What we can do, I believe, is to reverse the aphorism that 'language is the house of being' and essay the tentative hypothesis that our very self-conscious awareness of ourselves and the world is the Underived First Principle of which Plato spoke (*The Republic*, VI, 510B).

This is a conclusion that seems to me, at any rate, to be suggested by a consideration of the character of some of the key ideas that are commonly called metaphorical but also seem to be common to all cultures. For example, just as Lukes (1977) maintains that there are some criteria of rationality that are universal — for instance, the principles of identity and non-contradiction; just as Chomsky (1965, pp. 28–9) argues that some features of language — the formal rules for transformation — are culturally invariant; so the psychologists Clark and Clark (1978) believe that there are certain perceptions and capacities that are innate in all children, and that these are related to universals of language. Take the metaphor of 'possession' for example; this has to do with such fundamental perceptions as the infant's consciousness of his inalienable possession of his own body and all its predicates in spatial extension and time. This leads him/her to an awareness of boundaries to the 'here' and 'there' and 'now' and 'then' — all psychological 'primitives' that slowly extend themselves and are shown in our tendency to predicate in terms of such basic categorizations as space and time, the capacity for locomotion and hence power, nearness and possession; and in the primitives of attraction/repulsion and measure that lead on to the metaphors of *value*. And there are primitive and universal perceptions, too. Bollinger summarizes the Clarks well:

> There are certain 'best' colours for the human visual systems; these are noted first, and all languages are found to have names for them in proportion to how good the human eye is in perceiving them . . . There are also 'best' shapes — the open shapes of line and curve, and the closed shapes of square and circle . . . And

there are natural dimensions. Verticality is one, which the child perceives as the pull of gravity . . .

> Other spatial perceptions include *here* and *there*, where hereness involves contact — with the mother for example — and thereness involves the opposite. There is probably a primitive notion of *thingness* — of constancy in an object. . . . Further, as two things or happenings occur regularly in close succession, a basis is laid for *cause* and *effect*. All languages reflect these perceptions in their most basic categories. And this is simply to say that as children learn to speak they learn at the same time to draw comparisons, to cast the net of their language wide enough to bring in new experiences and class them under old rubrics. (Bollinger, 1980, p. 141 ff.)

The same thesis regarding human perception and cognition, transcendentally deduced by Kant with his synthetic *a priori* categories of the understanding, is here advanced as a tentative scientific hypothesis by two empirical psychologists, as a result of their investigation and analysis of the growth of children's perception and the increasingly complex and sophisticated developments of their capacity to classify and categorize their experiences of themselves and the world in which they live. The arguments are, of course, different, but whether metaphysical or empirical the conclusion is the same: there is a universality about human language and the power to conceptualize, that is a function of certain features that are basic to all human perceptions of ourselves and our environment and, whether we describe these as being fixed in time, space, quantity, quality, modality and relation; or based on colour, spatial extension, natural dimensions and substance, the outcome is the same. It is that there are certain fixed points that are the ground of all our appraisals of our reality, and these have to do, as I believe, with our common experience of spatio-temporal extension that provides us with a persisting principle of consciousness and a permanent point of reference — a touchstone against which all further extensions of ourselves and our capacity to communicate our awareness of our situation can be measured. *Pace* Sapir and Whorf, the aborigine may have no concept of a Cadillac or an electron, but, as Cooper (1973, ch. 5) humorously remarks, they would soon know it if they fell over one or were affected by it. The metaphors which they would employ to express their fear, pain and disgust might be ones that were relative to their own culture but metaphors of language they would be nonetheless; for all our linguistic articulation, it seems to me, is derived from and rooted in the small set of ways in which human experience and understanding is classified. Hannah Arendt puts it in this way:

> The categories and ideas of human reason have their ultimate source in the human senses and, all conceptual or metaphysical language is actually and strictly

metaphorical. Moreover, the human brain which supposedly does our thinking is as terrestrial, earth bound, as any other part of the human body. It was precisely by abstracting from these terrestrial conditions, by appealing to a power of imagination and abstraction that would, as it were, lift the human mind out of the gravitational field of the earth and look down upon it from some point in the universe, that modern science reached its most glorious and, at the same time, most baffling achievements. (Arendt, 1963)

Our language and conceptualizing capacities are built upon and develop from the most fundamental features of our being human, of which perhaps the ones of which we are most sharply aware are our vulnerability and our mortality. This, at least, is common — though it is not the only thing. As Bollinger puts it:

> If all that we can know and talk about is ultimately in terms of something else, and that in turn is shaped by childhood gropings for connections grounded firmly enough in impressions of space, touch, size, motion, direction and balance to hold them steady and enable an uncertain mind to grasp them, then our assurances come more from finding that our reality is shared by others than from the security of its own anchors. Metaphor is at work, but it has been at work in the past and brings to us a world to some extent prefabricated in our language . . . (Bollinger, 1980, p. 145)

A point also made by W.V. Quine (1979):

> Metaphor, or something like it, governs both the growth of our language and our acquisition of it.

Some might have a distaste for this kind of metaphysics and be unconvinced by it. They might reasonably maintain that it still avoids the problem of giving an account of the extra, and more subtle, types and dimensions of meaning that are typically found in the works of poets and playwrights; they might argue that its connection with education is tenuous; and they might claim that a consequence of the kind of view advanced above would be that one could say of all language that it is metaphorical. To say so much would, of course, be mistaken; as D.M. Taylor points out:

> such a conclusion would deprive the word 'metaphorical' of a specific sense, hence deprive *that* conclusion of any content. (Taylor, D.M., 1970, p. 170)

What specific sense we give to metaphorical usage must therefore be explained, if we are to end by giving some account of the role and function of metaphor in educational discourse, apart from what has been said already about children's learning of language (of which the educational implications should be obvious).

One way of making progress in giving some account of the power and persuasiveness of metaphorical locution is, I believe, to adopt and follow up the distinction drawn by Donald Davidson between what words *mean* and what words are *used for*. Metaphor, he argues, is a linguistic device which is legitimate

> not only in literature but in science, philosophy and the law; it is effective in praise and abuse, prayer and promotion, description and prescription . . . metaphor belongs exclusively to the domain of use. It is something brought off by the imaginative employment of words and sentences and depends entirely on the ordinary or literal meanings of those words and hence of the sentences they comprise. (Davidson 1978, p. 32)

In other words, metaphorical locution is a kind of 'persuasive definition': it is a particular kind of 'speech act' which comes off, or fails to come off, in proportion to the hearer's understanding of and familiarity with the kinds of meaning defined by the demands of the context in which the utterance is issued. In this respect metaphors are like jokes — or lies: they meet, or fail to meet, with 'uptake' in terms of the hearer;[8] and, in accordance with the hearer's knowledge of language, receptivity and imagination, so their utterance is more or less 'happy'.

In the bringing-off of metaphor key factors will be the intentions of the speaker (since it is only these, as Davidson points out, that differentiate a statement like 'she is a witch' into metaphor or lie); the context in which the utterance takes place (Wittgenstein 1953, para. 583: 'What is happening now has significance. The surroundings give a word its importance.'); and the sensitivity and imagination of the receiver (there would be much missed by those who would take an expression like 'Sleep knits up the ravelled sleeve of care' *au pied de la lettre*). That is why metaphor is similar to lying in perlocutionary effect: it is what it prompts us to think, see or imagine that is important, what it promotes and evokes in us by the particular concatenation of unusual terms of which it is constituted. It provokes an 'arrest', which, the speaker hopes, will precipitate a *disclosure*.

Some metaphors in education have become so widely employed, of course, that they have slowly lost all power to act in this way; they have become clichés that gradually become standard terms in our ordinary discourse in it. This, I suspect, has been the fate of such expressions as 'education as initiation' (Peters, 1965).[9] But the insights called forth and activated by that metaphor were once new and startling: at the time when it was first uttered, this particular innovation was an exemplification of a new and creative imagination at work in the field in question — like that of those physicists who call one of the behaviours of a sub-atomic particle 'Charm'. It is a caution to us to note that the newly-coined metaphor that was arresting in December 1963 (when Peters delivered his inaugural lecture) quickly became a mindless slogan that was taken up as the badge of an orthodoxy, against which any kind of dissent was discouraged by its mere repetition. And that is one use of metaphorical expression of which we should be most aware: that certain metaphors, in education as elsewhere (and nowhere perhaps more than in politics), function so as to give the finality of an incontestable pronouncement to an idea, with which, it is tacitly and cunningly assumed, everyone is familiar and agrees. 'Child-centred education', 'education for citizenship', 'teacher accountability' — in certain hands and certain quarters these are certainly used (whether consciously or not) as 'fixers', as 'thought-stoppers'. And such is the power of this feature of language use that, all too often, they succeed. Sadly, that seems to be nowhere more true than in education, in which dead metaphor, slogan, cliché, and mindless jargon of this kind, thrive. And our readiness to get entangled in that kind of talk, or our carelessness in avoiding it, will lead us only too rapidly into the thickest parts of the 'tropical jungle' of which Quine speaks, that still disfigures much of the less drily rigorous and scientific areas of educational discourse.

There is, however, another possibility: a more positive use of metaphorical expression which resides in its *innovative* and creative power. As Davidson remarks, it is part of the business of metaphor to promote unexpected or subtle parallels or analogies. Metaphors encapsulate and put forward proposals for another way of looking at things and of grasping inchoate intimations of possibilities, giving voice to meanings that are shifting, elusive, unstable, polymorphous and illusory, and never more so than in some worlds where Quine's drily literal cognitive discourse is alien: the worlds of poetry and the arts. In these realms — but also in others: science, philosophy, the law, politics and education — metaphors help us the better to strive towards grasping the visions and truths of their artificers and attempting, however imperfectly, to share in them. Ricoeur (1978) talks of the 'rule of metaphor' in this connection and reminds us that living metaphor constantly returns to present conceptual thinking with the possibility of the re-presentation and re-newal of the life of reason. The creative imagination works in and through metaphor and presents us with an increased awareness of alternative possible worlds.

Metaphor is classically based on the distinctions between those predicates that belong to a subject and those that do not. The role of metaphor, on this thesis, is well caught by Nelson Goodman:

> . . . a metaphor is an affair between a predicate with a past and an object that yields while protesting. (Goodman, 1968, pp. 69–70)

Clearly, normative notions of 'propriety', 'fittingness', 'suitability', and so on, arise here and show the grip that the long-fixed agreements of language have on our creative and imaginative powers. Maybe that is why traditionalists feel uncomfortable in the presence of novel uses in unpredictable places; Wittgenstein (1953, para. 38) warned that 'philosophical problems arise when language goes on holiday' — when things are not 'in their proper place'.

But the stricter interpretation of this aphorism would make philosophy have a 'policing' role over language, a view with which Wittgenstein, who held that 'philosophy leaves everything as it is', would have strongly disagreed. Language *is* the 'house of our being'; some of us inhabit dwellings very strange, but nevertheless capable of entry by other language-users. Derrida reminds us that metaphor is a species of linguistic play in which we invite others to join, so that they too may see how fertile and productive of insights and illuminations it can be. What we are trying to do in our use of metaphor is to see how far we can transform language and reconstruct it, though only *pro tempore* and for particular purposes. To be 'invaded' by metaphor is to be surrounded by semantic play; to stay in it is to be fixed into permanent displacement and to head for that kind of mindlessness or madness that only the utterly pedestrian or the divinely-inspired artist can know.

A good model for assessing the utility and appropriateness of metaphors in educational discourse — those that are not already lifeless clichés or bureaucratic jargon, that is — is thus that which applies an external criterion to them. The best of these, in my view, is one derived from Popper and Lakatos — that of fertility, productivity of new insights and fresh illuminations on old themes and explanatory power. Though some educational metaphors, on this criterion, will be degenerating ('education for democracy', 'equality of opportunity' and the like) others may still have much to offer us, however great our distaste for them on other grounds. Why not 'education for accountability', after all? Metaphor may be, as Cohen (1981) regards it, the favourite child of the marriage of memory and imagination; but, as any paediatrician will tell us, children need a varied and increasing diet of fresh *pabulum* if they are to thrive and continue to flourish. Without continual re-appraisal, critical examination and re-interpretation, our choicest and most innovative metaphors will quickly stagnate and die. Maybe the 'secret-garden' of the curriculum is now looking more like jungle than cultivated clearing; but it may be, too, that a critical and creative thinker like Denis Lawton will appear soon and pro-duce a fresh proposal for our judgement, reinterpretation, and acceptance and thus re-define the boundaries of our thinking on that issue.

This activity of proposal and re-interpretation is the one that is at the heart of all metaphorizing, according to Davidson. In both fabricating, giving voice to and responding to metaphor, we are attempting 'to evoke what the metaphor brings to our attention . . .' The point about this particular language use is 'that there is no limit to what it calls to our attention . . . When we try to say what a metaphor "means", we soon realize there is no end to what we want to mention . . .'

This, of course, is where education comes in; there is as much room for the explanation and elaboration of the multi-vocality of metaphor as there is for very many other speech acts. As Davidson prompts us:

> Many of us need help if we are to see what the author of a metaphor wanted us to see, and what a more sensitive or educated reader grasps.

In this respect the teacher of any subject has a greater power and respon-sibility than any mere critic or interpreter might enjoy; for he can open up fresh worlds of significance to minds that have not yet had those visions that he himself has been vouchsafed or enjoyed the subtlety and exquisiteness of the effects that their intimations and evocations have had upon him. Like no one else the teacher of physics, of history, of geography and of the arts can sensitize his pupils and add, as rich increments to and expansions of their consciousness, the beauties, refinements and complexities that are instantiated in every living metaphor in our language. And this is as true of educational discourse as it is of models in science, analogies in history and metaphors in poetry: for the illuminations that creative innovations in this kind of language use provide and suggest can throw a fresh and often more searching light on to those areas of our talk that are still overshadowed by the jungle of misunderstandings that much of its mindless chatter and self-confident jargonizing can create. By thoughtful use of the instrument that is metaphor in education we can do much to lighten that darkness.

Let the final words be those of Davidson:

> Metaphor is the dreamwork of language, and like all dreamwork its inter-pretation reflects as much on the interpreter as on the originator. The inter-

pretation of dreams requires collaboration between a dreamer and a waker, even if they be the same person; and the act of interpretation is itself a work of the imagination. So, too, understanding a metaphor is as much a creative endeavour as making a metaphor, and as little guided by rules. (Davidson, 1978, p. 31)

That collaboration, that imaginative interplay, that kind of understanding, is the goal of the teacher of every subject. It is the stuff of which education, at least in my conception of it, is made.

Notes

1. In *The Republic* (VI and VII) Plato explains what he means by 'the highest kind of knowledge' by three similes — that of the Sun (505A–509C), the Divided Line (509C–511E) and the Allegory of the Cave (514A–521B).
2. Cf. *inter alia* Gellner (1959), Ch. II, section 4; and Popper (1972), pp. 123–4 and 194 ff. for a rehearsal of some of the main points of criticism of this view.
3. Wittgenstein (1953), paras. 7, 81, 83, 182 and 19–23; though against all this cf. Gellner (1959), Ch. II, section 8.
4. Wittgenstein (1953), para. 43. Cf. also his query (ibid. para. 20): '. . . doesn't the fact that sentences have the same sense consist in their having the same use?' Cf. also Ryle, G. (1963 p. 120): 'Understanding a word or phrase is knowing how to use it, i.e. make it perform its role in a wide range of sentences'. For some important qualifications on this see Cooper (1973), Chs. 2, sections 4 and 8, section 3.
5. Lewis Carroll (1887), *Through the Looking Glass.* London: Macmillan, p. 114 (Ch. VI):
   'When *I* use a word,' Humpty Dumpty said in rather a scornful tone, 'it means just what I choose it to mean — neither more nor less.'
   'The question is,' said Alice, 'whether you *can* make words mean different things.'
   'The question is,' said Humpty Dumpty, 'which is to be master — that's all.'
6. Waismann (1965), Ch. XIII, 'Structural descriptions', and p. 176 ff. on 'metaphor'.
7. Cf. Cooper (1973), pp. 84–5; Searle (1969), Ch. II sections 6 and 7 *passim*; and Cooper (1972).
8. Cf. Austin (1962) *passim*, but especially Lecture I, p. 4 ff.
9. 'Education as initiation' was the title of R.S. Peters' inaugural lecture in the Chair of the Philosophy of Education at the University of London Institute of Education. The lecture was delivered in December 1963, and later amended and reprinted (Peters, 1965).

Chapter Three
Metaphor, Imagination and Conceptions of Education
R.K. Elliott

When I first began to think about metaphor in education with a view to writing this paper I felt a bias in favour of educational metaphor, and hoped to be able to show that metaphor plays an important role in educational theory. It seemed to me that the strongest case I could possibly make in favour of metaphor would be by showing that educational theory is based on a single ineliminable metaphor, as is Husserlian phenomenology, in which the notion of intentionality has to be introduced as a directedness, a pointing towards, or the beaming of a ray of light towards something. But nothing of this sort, implicit in every thought and discoverable by introspective reflection, is available as the essential basis of education. Theories of learning are dependent on metaphors, because they are centrally concerned either with mental acts and conscious processes or with the operations of mental mechanisms below the level of consciousness, all of which are describable only by metaphorical means. But examining the bases of learning seems to lead away from education rather than towards it. Philosophers of education, when they ask what education is, are not asking what learning is or how it occurs, but what things ought to be learnt, and for the sake of what. This suggests that the metaphor or metaphors of the kind I am expecting to find especially important will identify education with a process or activity of some sort or other, and will indicate, immediately or remotely, some end or a general class of ends to which this process, etc., is necessarily or normally directed.

In the course of its history, educational theory has provided a number of metaphors which fit this specification. Among them are some which are still widely known and used, such as that of education as formation or production; as preparation or apprenticeship; as initiation; as guidance; as growth; as liberation. Each presupposes that education has a point or purpose, and each is normative in character, indicating what education ought to be by seeming to state, incompletely, what it essentially is. For the sake of convenience I shall refer to these particular metaphors as 'the educational metaphors' or 'the metaphors of education', not thereby intending to suggest that they are the only ones which offer to disclose the essence of education, or the commonest, or the most worthy of attention.

Metaphors are widely used in educational discussion and fulfil a variety of functions, such as introducing fresh perspectives, making illuminating comparisons and contrasts, picking out kinds of phenomena not yet named, emphasis, illustration, enlivening dull writing, and many others. The vast majority of such metaphors are only transient waves in the sea of everyday educational reflection. Even when some lasting achievement is accomplished by their means, they themselves die and are forgotten. The metaphors of education, though not of a different species from these ephemeral metaphors, make a contribution of a different kind. But it is not clear exactly what it is. It must be admitted that at first glance the list of metaphors of education induces an oppressive sense of the banal.

When we ask concerning the meaning of these metaphors, their incompleteness and therefore ambiguity becomes apparent. If education is preparation, for example, it may be preparation for life, or for work, or for war, or for prayer and the love of one's neighbour. If it is initiation, it may be initiation into a society through learning its values and practices, or into a religious community through learning its rituals and articles of faith, or into something different again. If it is liberation, it may be from cultural domination, or from ignorance, or from passions and prejudices, or from other things. Every education might claim to be guidance, but different educational theories have different ideas about what counts as guidance. Every education might claim that it brings about growth, but the theories differ in their conceptions of growth. Similarly, even progressively educated people are said to be 'formed' by their education and to be 'products' of it. Because of this ambiguity it may seem that the metaphors of education, though extensively used in educational discourse, do not play any specially significant or very stable part in it. Their incompleteness makes them flexible instruments for communication, but they lack depth. It is not because of their versatility that they have become prominent in educational discourse, however, so much as by virtue of their connection with certain well-known theories of education, for as well as having a free untrammelled use, they are also used in a way such that their interpretation is bound to the theory (or type of theory) of education with which they are most closely associated, and to which, in some cases, they might be said to belong.

It is sometimes taken for granted that metaphors like 'initiation' and the rest are now dead. Although they may have been important once, when they were alive and had the capacity to startle and disturb, their importance is now a thing of the past. This estimate has an intuitive appeal, and there is certainly some justification for it. 'Education is initiation', for example, can be, and may need to be, a living metaphor if used without reference to any particular theory. Among professional educationalists, however, it is often used merely as a means of referring either to R.S. Peters' theory in particular (Peters, 1964/5), or to the more general point of view which his theory exemplifies (see Aspin, ch. 2 of this volume). In many professional contexts, a person who wanted to declare his adherence to Peters' theory could effectively do so by saying 'Education is, of course, initiation.' Used in this way, simply as a means of referring to theories with which they are associated, the educational metaphors satisfy all but the most stringent criteria of metaphorical death. It is true that they do not *need* to be living metaphors in order to do the work of names, but it would be disappointing if that were the only special function they have acquired through their association with the educational theories. In their free use, their functions are not significantly different from those of other 'ephemeral' metaphors; in their tied use, they do have a special function, which prolongs their moribund existence, but it is not one of a particularly noteworthy or impressive kind. It could still be said of them that each serves to draw attention to some aspect or character of education, as we ordinarily use the word, or to something which has a claim to be called education; but it would be the theories associated with the metaphors, rather than the ambiguous metaphors themselves, which isolate and emphasize the aspects or characters concerned.

The importance of the metaphors would be established if it could be shown that through their connection with the theories they perform a function like that performed by explanatory models in science. This hope, also, is ill-founded. Only two of the metaphors — initiation and growth — incorporate analogies which it seems might be sufficiently definitely structured, and might admit of sufficiently detailed relevant development, to be suitable as explanatory models of the process of education generally. Of these two, that of growth is far the more promising. There are not one but two metaphors connected with growth theory, the growth metaphor proper and the 'horticultural' metaphor. The former can be cast as: 'Education *qua* learning is mental growth which is biological growth'.

The 'horticultural' metaphor has the form: 'Education *qua* teaching is tending biological growth'. Growth theorists have themselves elaborated the horticultural analogy, but it seems unlikely that they 'discovered' from it anything of which they were not already convinced:[1] that the child needs to be protected from traditions, conventions and authorities as a growing plant needs to be protected from frost, pests and browsing cattle; that the child needs to be given plenty of opportunity for learning as the plant needs dung and water; or that forcing the intellectual development of the child tends to be detrimental to him, as forcing their growth tends to be detrimental to plants. It seems that the analogy was developed to rationalize preferred educational practices rather than to discover what practices there should be. Nevertheless, in the idea that the life and growth of both plant and child are effects of manifestations of one and the same nature, growth theory provides something like a theoretical bridge between the idea of growth and education. This seems to give the growth metaphor something of the character of a scientific model, redeeming it from being a mere literary device, or an arbitrary means of introducing practices towards which the theories are favourably predisposed.

The growth metaphor has recently been much criticized, most destructively on the ground that criteria of mental (intellectual, emotional, moral and spiritual) growth and maturity are relative to different cultures and even to individual philosophers, and cannot conceivably be the end of any merely natural process. This criticism seems fatal to growth theory in so far as it relies confusedly upon normative conceptions of growth and maturity. To the extent that it avoids presupposing conventional criteria, however, it tends to pass over into a pure libertarian theory, for which growth, however conceived, is no longer the primary end of education, its place being taken by non-violation of the child's freedom and the protection of its individual integrity. It could be said that in its highly developed 'libertarian' version the basic educational insight of growth theory — that education is an art of tendance — is preserved, and its limitations recognized and accepted. But when the theory is so interpreted it can no longer claim that it is because plants and children are alike creatures of nature that the education of children ought to be like the tendance of plants. Its position is that the education of children ought to be like the tending of plants because making children satisfy conventional standards is a violation of their autonomy. If education is an art of tendance only, it is because the educators prefer non-violation of freedom above other values. The growth metaphor *is* an arbitrary means of introducing favoured practices, and does not function as a scientific or *quasi*-scientific model. This does not mean ˴

that growth theory is inferior to other theories, but that it is not superior to them in this particular respect.

Contemporary initiation theories were not constructed by developing the analogy between initiation and education, and do not contain even an implicit claim that the initiation metaphor functions like a scientific model. It is not argued, for example, that there ought to be examinations in schools because primitive tribes subject initiation candidates to ordeals, or because religious authorities subject confirmation candidates to tests. In so far as they think metaphorically of initiation at all, contemporary theorists think of it not as a rite but as the often prolonged process of preparation which typically precedes the celebration of the rite, a process which is itself education, as we ordinarily use the word. The development of the analogy, if it were carried out, would be an exercise in the comparative study of education, from which something might be learnt, perhaps, about the scope of the ordinary concept of education. But trying to find out what education is by comparing and contrasting independent instances of it would not be a case of using a metaphor like a scientific model.

Whereas modern initiation theorists do not elaborate the analogy between education and initiation, Plato did — not the analogy between education (*qua* schooling) and the initiation process which is itself an education, but that between the entire educational process as he conceived it (from its beginning in blind ignorance to its culmination in the vision of the Good) and a particular initiation rite. In her book *Themis* Jane Harrison remarks:

> We are told again and again that Plato 'borrowed much of his imagery' from the mysteries, but it is not external borrowing of a mere illustration. Plato's whole scheme alike of education and philosophy is but an attempted rationalization of the primitive mysticism of initiation, and most of all that profound and perennial mysticism of the central *rite de passage*, the death and the new birth, social, moral, intellectual. (Harrison, 1963, p. 513.)

As Jane Harrison suggests by emphasizing the *mysticism* of the rite, it is hardly conceivable that the rite could have been central to Plato's philosophy and educational theory unless before making a metaphorical use of it he had already understood the significance attached to it by the Orphists themselves. The details of the rite are obscure, but it seems that candidates had to endure a descent into darkness, from which they were eventually brought forth again into the light. No doubt the symbolism was of death and rebirth, but also of corruption and purification, and of salvation, since, if Plato is a trustworthy authority, the Orphists believed that the unjust are plunged into a slough in Hades. These ideas were undoubtedly of great significance of Plato. He writes, in connection with training in the method of dialectic:

> When the eye of the soul is sunk in the veritable slough of barbarous ignorance, this method gently draws it forth and guides it upwards, assisted in this work of conversion by the arts I have enumerated. (*The Republic*, 533d)

The 'arts' to which Plato is referring are the mathematical sciences, the function of which in his educational scheme is to facilitate the learner in separating the intelligible Forms from every trace of sense, an achievement which is extremely difficult because of the body's stubborn and powerful yearning for the objects of its senses. Mathematical study is a purification of the soul, and much depends on it, for if it fails and the learner remains in the slough, unable to separate the Good and the other Forms from the mud of the senses, '. . . he will dream away his life here in a sleep which has no awakening on this side of that world of Death where he will sleep for ever' (*The Republic*, 534c). These grim words were meant to create fear, but associated with the threat of perdition is a promise of felicity. By education the noblest, imperishable faculty of the soul can be freed from the domination of the appetites and led up towards the contemplation of the highest of all realities (*The Republic*, 532c).

The insight fundamental to Plato's philosophy is that knowledge is the good for man. The insight fundamental to his educational theory is that the good education is the one which makes the learner capable of achieving knowledge. The knowledge in question is not the wisdom of the Orphists, whatever that might have been, but knowledge of the kind which Socrates sought in vain and perhaps believed to be unattainable. Plato expresses these insights by using the initiation rite, rich with its own mythic significance, as a complex metaphor of education. The metaphor did not enable Plato himself to discover what education was — to suppose that would be to forget Socrates. But it may record the intelligible content of an experience of conversion or commitment, if at some time Plato came to see that getting knowledge of the Forms is of the highest importance for the individual soul, and that not to get it is a spiritual disaster; and if this came about through his imaginatively identifying the philosophical life with the progress of the soul as represented in the initiation rite. The identification, if it happened, may well have been precipitated by the affective quality of the symbolism of the rite, which would have been consonant with Plato's own feeling towards the getting and not getting of philosophical knowledge. In the experience of conversion, the intelligible content of the symbolism would have undergone a metaphorical transposition, Orphist perdition not being in the same key as Platonic perdition, Orphist felicity as Platonic felicity, though in each case the thought of the one was a source of terror and of the other a source of joy.

These speculations may not be entirely accurate, but they provide a clue to the nature of the function of the initiation metaphor. The metaphor is not necessary for the discovery or the exposition of the strictly philosophical content of Plato's theory, or for the detailed exposition of his ideal curriculum. Plato himself accomplishes the work of exposition, entirely in plain speech, in the central books of *The Republic*. Whatever the function of the metaphor is, it is not much like that of a scientific model. If its function were only to re-present the abstract philosophical content in visual symbolism, it would be a surprisingly primitive ornament for Plato to have attached to his austere and refined thought. It is something much more than an ornament because by means of it certain moral and religious ideas associated with Orphic initiation are applied to education, their sense undergoing a shift in the process. It can be said, therefore, that the metaphor is part of the complex system of means which Plato employs for communicating the existential import of this thought concerning education.

The chief importance of the metaphors of education, generally, lies in their rhetorical function, which is to stimulate imagination, to arouse feeling, and to prompt action. This may make it sound as if the use of the educational metaphors in philosophical contexts is inappropriate. If so, it should be remembered that education is a practical endeavour, concerned about individual and collective good and with the preservation and transmission of values, and that educational theorists usually address themselves to persons practically engaged with education in one capacity or another. A philosopher who recommends teachers to change the character of the ends they are pursuing, or to see them in a different perspective, is asking them, in effect, to modify their opinions concerning what is good, and to re-assess to some extent the value of their past life and work. One would expect him, out of respect for them, and in solidarity with them as he wants them to become, to address them in a manner which shows his own concern for the values he is recommending. Plato could not even have expressed his *meaning* unequivocally in a piece of purely technical work done in the cool manner of an intellectual exercise.

A further relevant consideration is that persons such as teachers who have taken it upon themselves to pursue the good over a long period, through fair and ill fortune, stand in need of inspiration. Kant recognizes this in his *Religion*, when he acknowledges that we cannot help asking what is to come of all this moral endeavour of ours. He acknowledges that besides duty, which commands our respect, we need something to love, a vision of the end we are working towards, and conceives this end as a state of affairs in which every person in morally perfect and happy in proportion to his merit, the *Summum Bonum* (Kant, 1960). If, when dealing with matters of great existential significance, Kant and Plato did not think it inappropriate to stimulate the feelings and imagination of their readers, ought we to conclude that their attitudes were not properly philosophical?

Kant's work throws light not only on the inspirational function of the metaphors of education, but also on the nature of the evocativeness upon which their inspirational power depends. In the *Critique of Judgement* he maintains that beauty can be called the expression of aesthetic Ideas (Meredith, 1952, p. 183). By an 'aesthetic Idea' he means, roughly speaking, an imaginatively evocative image. A poet, for example, has a mental image — an imaginative presentation of a particular concept — which evokes in him a wealth of additional thought and images in what Kant describes as 'the rapid and transient play of the imagination' (Meredith, p. 180). The poet's task is to find a form of words which will communicate the image in such a manner that it will induce a similar 'rapid and transient play' in the reader.[2]

An educational metaphor is not an image which presents a concept, however, but a concept with which another concept, that of education, is identified. This difference between educational metaphor and aesthetic Idea seems crucial for, because a wealth of significance can be encapsulated in an image, the degree of evocativeness possible for an image far exceeds that which is possible for a bare concept. The difference is not so crucial, because not so absolute as it seems. In an educational metaphor, the other nature with which education is identified may be conceived in relatively general and abstract terms, or in relatively particular, concrete terms. Liberation, for example, may be represented abstractly as the freeing of someone in general from something in general; or much more concretely, as (for example) the freeing of a bound prisoner from his bonds and from the cave or dungeon in which he is imprisoned. In this latter case, the general idea of education is identified with the image. The idea of education is thereby given a sensous, pictorial, existence and the image, which already symbolizes liberation, becomes secondarily a symbol of education. The image retains its original significance, of course, together with whatever associations, ideational and affective, it originally had.

The original evocativeness of the image, enlivened by the tension created by the identification of the image with the idea of education, is one of the main sources of the evocativeness of the educational metaphors, all of which make use of images. In the Platonic example, the initiation metaphor involves an image which is as concrete and as evocative as many great poetic images. The horticultural metaphor is associated with an image which is as detailed and concrete, if not so poetic, as that of the initiation rite. The guidance metaphor has available to it images which have been highly evocative since the earliest times. When the idea of liberation is thought reflectively, it commonly receives imaginative fulfilment in an inner spontaneous enactment of a bursting forth or breaking out from an imaginary state of indeterminate constriction into a state of freedom. This imagining of liberation 'from within' could be regarded as an image of one's own liberation, though it is not given so particular a meaning by the person imagining it. The image has a strong affective aspect, and is commonly present also when liberation is thought through the symbolism of some more detailed image, such as that of the freeing of a prisoner from a cave.

A second main source of the evocativeness of the educational metaphors is their reference to theory. An educational metaphor may be evocative to some degree without reference to any particular theory, but it can become much more richly evocative when thought with reference to the theory to which it belongs, and to the moral, political and metaphysical ideas upon which the theory depends — ideas which are themselves highly evocative. Its association with all these ideas is not merely accidental, but thematic. Proximately or remotely, they are germane to it.

Unfortunately, our awareness that the educational metaphors have this reference to theory, together with our deep respect for scientific methods, may have inclined us to misconceive their function. In a metaphor the concepts identified remain nevertheless distinct. This identity-in-difference is possible only because there exists an analogy, or in certain special cases a simple affinity, between the terms. Where there is an analogy, as is the case with the educational metaphors, it is capable of being worked out in detail. The working out is done to a certain extent, though not explicitly, if the nature identified with education is symbolized in a detailed image. Conversely, when the working out of the analogy is done explicitly, it produces what is, in effect, a more detailed image. If the elaboration of the horticultural analogy can safely be taken as a standard — which I believe it can because of the difference in type between educational and scientific theories (see Hirst, 1972) — the explicit development of the analogy implicit in an educational metaphor, though it may be conceived as putting the metaphor to a use like that of an explanatory model, owes whatever *legitimate* effectiveness it has to the image which it creates, and that effectiveness is rhetorical rather than theoretical.

It is possible to distinguish, in a Kantian manner, the metaphor as educational Idea, which is the evocative thought of education as initiation, or as whatever other nature it is metaphorically identified with, from the metaphor as *expression* of an education Idea, which is the experience of some form of words — some sentence or system of related sentences — as communicating the educational Idea. The same Idea can be expressed in many different ways, barely or elaborately, inventively or in a stereotyped manner, etc.

A third source of the evocativeness of the educational metaphors, or of their lack of it, is the form of their expression. I have suggested that in a particular expression an educational Idea may have an evocativeness which rivals that of a poetic image. There are, however, certain further differences between educational and aesthetic Ideas which have a bearing on this matter. First, our attitude in experiencing an educational Idea is normally practical rather than disinterested, as a result of which questions of truth and falsity are crucial in connection with educational Ideas, whereas they are usually irrelevant from an aesthetic point of view. The suspicion of falsity can still the reverberation of an educational metaphor. Secondly, in an educational Idea the play of imagination is not entirely free, because the connection of the educational Idea with a particular theory of education largely determines which additional ideas are associated with education in the educational Idea. They can seem fixed, massive and inert, beyond imagination's power to quicken. Finally, very often the form in which an educational Idea is expressed is undistinguished, with the result that the expressions do not have the resonance — and therefore not the beauty — of truly poetic images. For all these reasons, an educational metaphor may depress rather than inspire us, demanding from us a response which we cannot spontaneously make. For those who do not flatly reject his philosophy as false, Plato's initiation metaphor can still be intensely evocative, nevertheless, and they are likely to find it more rather than less profoundly evocative if they have an interest in education. But whereas for educational writing to elicit a response comparable to that given to a successful work of art it must itself have artistic quality, persons committed to a particular educational theory normally find metaphorical references to it evocative to a certain degree. Even when a metaphorical expression of an educational Idea is used apparently only for the purpose of making a reference to a theory, it makes the reference by reminding the reader of a fundamental aim of the theory and so still has some slight inspirational power. It is when a writer tries to do something more ambitious, more demanding of his readers, that he runs the risk of serious failure. Then, though he need not have artistic genius comparable to Plato's, he does need to choose his words carefully, lest he inflict upon his readers a stultifying experience of the banal.

The point needs emphasizing that the imaginative power of an educational metaphor is not left unaffected if the theory with which it is associated has been, or is believed to have been, refuted or subjected to serious unanswered criticism. It is now very widely believed that Plato's fundamental philosophy is based on certain erroneous presuppositions, a belief which if it is true makes the theory of Forms untenable and thereby deprives the initiation metaphor of all point. It is incredible that Plato's theory should retain its appeal on the strength of its rhetoric alone, especially when its rhetorical superstructure is so deeply and subtly related to its philosophical foundations. The fate which has overtaken the Platonic metaphor of initiation is that of decline into a thing of merely literary beauty, as which it is now free to inspire a true poetic state, a rapid and transient play of imagination which is sheer delight and refreshment to the disinterested mind. But it does not have the depth or imperative force which it would have if the Platonic philosophy were believed to be valid, or more or less valid, or thought to have a chance of validity. In short, it is no longer taken seriously, but read as literature. In this case the aesthetic Idea lives the death of the educational Idea.

Contemporary initiation theory, though still bearing a resemblance to Plato's version of the theory, is not encumbered with his realist metaphysic, and therefore not with his extreme views concerning the nature of knowledge and the outcome of education. Since the items discarded were a basis of the appeal of the initiation metaphor as used by Plato, questions arise concerning the nature of the imaginative appeal of the metaphor as used by the contemporary philosophers, and concerning the nature of the appeal of the contemporary version of the theory itself.

In his inaugural lecture *Education as Initiation* Peters (1964) expressly uses the word 'initiation' in a very general sense, to cover transactions by which people get on the inside of worthwhile public forms of life. Education is initiation because it is getting children inside a particular class of worthwhile traditions, namely distinct forms of theoretical and practical knowledge. As Peters uses it, the 'initiation metaphor', if that is what it is, is logically on a par with an expression like 'Man is an animal', in which a genus to which a species belongs is predicated of that species. In such cases, the expression is metaphorical only if, on receipt of it, people would normally entertain the idea of there being no significant difference between the species referred to and other species of the same genus, and would take it that the maker of the metaphorical remark did *not* intend simply to indicate what the genus was. Peters' use of 'initiation' satisfies neither of these criteria, and he cannot properly be said to use it metaphorically. He goes on to say that children 'start off in the position of the barbarians outside the gates. The problem is to get them inside the citadel of civilization so that they will understand and love what they see when they get there' (Peters, 1964, p. 43). The idea of education as the transformation of barbarians into civilized persons *is* metaphorical, but it is not an initiation metaphor. Neither is it a metaphor of *education*. Civilizing barbarians, like preparing the young for initiation, *is* an educational process. The metaphorical element in the 'civilizing' metaphor is the identification of one class of persons (schoolchildren) who are thought of as subjects of education with another such class (barbarians). 'Education as civilization' would have given a more accurate idea of the *point* of education according to Peters' theory. 'Education as initiation' seems to be a mere façade, since the apparent reference to tribal or religious practices performs no function whatever. But perhaps no such reference was intended. The literal meaning of 'initiation' is 'beginning', and if the word is taken as referring to forms of knowledge, 'education is initiation' accurately represents the *nature* of education, as Peters sees it. Be that as it may, he neither needs nor uses the initiation metaphor, and the imaginative appeal of his theory does not depend on it. Its appeal lies partly in his understanding of education as a civilizing endeavour, and partly in his respect for the traditions of knowledge. It is very much the same as that of other liberal theories, such as those of Matthew Arnold, and John Stuart Mill.

According to Oakeshott, education is 'initiation into an intellectual inheritance of great splendour and worth' (Oakeshott, 1975, p. 27). Here 'initiation' has presumably a religious reference, but it is the rest of the metaphor which is more noteworthy, in that it provides an example of imaginative fusion of the type where there is mutual transference of values between the terms of the metaphor. It would hardly seem necessary for splendour and worth — characteristic properties of gold — to be attributed metaphorically to forms of knowledge, since intellectuals, who constitute the audience Oakeshott is addressing, tend (at least intermittently) to believe that knowledge is *more* precious than gold. But the notion of treasure is made to shine with an intellectual and moral splendour, which is also, somehow, the splendour of gold. Listening to Oakeshott, have not we teachers already begun to think of ourselves as *guardians* of treasure? If by such means Oakeshott helps to renew the inspiration of teachers, it should not be assumed that he must be deceiving them, or threatening their rational autonomy. If we did not already believe that the intellectual heritage was precious, who could get us to love it by calling it a treasure? Similarly if, upon reflection, someone believes that, because of structures of domination in the arts and sciences, 'being initiated into forms of knowledge' is more like being made a slave than becoming a free citizen, it is unlikely that he will find inspiration from any of the metaphors used by initiation theorists.

In recent times, since it has come to be associated chiefly with the theories of Gramsci and Freire, the metaphor of liberation has proved perhaps the most stimulating of the educational metaphors. From the standpoint of our special concern with metaphor, Gramsci's work is more interesting than Freire's. Gramsci tends to see education primarily as a means to cultural and social liberation, only secondarily as a liberation in itself. He sees it as a liberation from superstition and prejudice, but this is educational liberation conceived in the familiar liberal humanist way (Hoare and Smith, 1971). Gramsci's perspective changes when he advocates the study of history in order that adult working class learners may come to understand the present social and political situation of their class through gaining an understanding of its historical genesis.[3] The achievement of social and political self-understanding could readily be seen not just as a means to, but as an actual beginning of, the cultural and social liberation of the working class. I have not been able to discover any instance of Gramsci's actually calling education 'liberation' in either of these senses. He writes of 'the struggle for hegemony in civil society', however, and his emphasis of the need for the working class to achieve hegemony (as moral and cultural leadership generally) is considered his most significant contribution to Marxist thought (Lawner, 1979, pp. 42–3). This idea of a struggle for working-class hegemony involves the idea of the liberation of the working class from direction by the class which is the leading one, and at least a general idea of means which could possibly be taken to that end. Gramsci writes, furthermore, that to understand one's adversary's position and reasons is 'to be liberated from the prison of ideologies in the bad sense of the word' and that 'sometimes one's adversary is the whole of past thought'. The idea expressed here is essentially similar to the idea of liberation through the attainment of social and political self-understanding, since that also is an idea of liberation from ideological determination. These considerations are sufficient, I believe, to justify the opinion that the liberation metaphor is expressed in Gramsci's writings.

Gramsci's work nevertheless raises the question whether a theory can rest on, or express, a metaphor if the metaphor is not explicitly formulated in it. Conceivably, there might be an analogy between education and some other thing (e.g. the liberation of a slave) which is discernible in the writings of an author like Gramsci but not expressed by him in metaphorical form, and it might be given explicit metaphorical expression by persons who read his work at some considerably later time. In such a case it would be too facile to assume that the metaphor was implied in the author's writings, for the metaphor is neither identical with the analogy nor logically derivable from it. If, however, we can satisfy ourselves that the author must have thought the educational Idea — as I have indicated can be done in Gramsci's case — this allows us to regard his writing as expressing the Idea; otherwise the most that could legitimately be said would be that the author was, or must have been, aware of the analogy. The case is different if the theory is considered as existing independently of its author, because this allows us to think of the theory as undergoing a process of development. Then when the metaphor is formulated explicitly we are able to say that it expresses what was already implicit in the theory at its earlier stage of development; but it was not 'implicit' in a logical sense, but only in the sense that awareness of an analogy commonly precedes the thinking and expression of the corresponding metaphorical idea.

The idea of education as guidance is not now fashionable, but has been historically important, especially in connection with spiritual education, whether religious or philosophical. The most influential historical source of this type of education is Socrates; the longest continuous tradition of it is to be found in Sufism. Characteristic of the type is a tendency to reduce the distance, to the point of eliminating it, between the terms of the pedagogical relation, viz. the teacher, the learner, and what is taught. To some extent and in some sense the teacher is himself the way: he is an eminent example of the state of wisdom or devotion, etc., to which he is attempting to bring the learner; and learning is essentially by imitating him. He may claim to speak with an authority derived through a tradition of discipleship from a prophetic source, or from some more direct contact with the divine (see Schimmel, 1975, pp. 101–5, 234–7). As regards his identification with the learner, he may direct his questioning entirely to getting the learner to articulate and clarify his ideas without contributing any positive idea of his own, or he may use devices such as irony and parable which, though they may bring the learner to the verge of insight, leave him to accomplish the insight by his own effort or commitment. Or he may speak or write in such a way that he becomes, as it were, a partner in the inner development of the learner's own thinking, seeming now like the voice of the learner's own everyday self, only more logical and honest, now like the voice of his conscience, only more subtle and inventive.

Teachers like Socrates and Kierkegaard exhibit both these major characteristics of the type, of which they are paradigms in the West. The idea fundamental to this conception of education is a commonplace one; being shown how to do or be something (guidance) is no more remarkable than, and hardly even distinct from, being taught the rules and other practices of some activity (initiation). The metaphorical element in initiation theory, and in the theories associated with the other educational metaphors, tends to be replaced, as the account of education is elaborated, by non-metaphorical specifications of objective activities, abilities and standards; but, in the same circumstances, the metaphorical element in the guidance conception of education intensifies. This happens because development of the account of education as guidance directs us not only to objective structures and ends, but also to the phenomena of existential communications, for the description of which metaphor is an essential means. Seeing these phenomena as instances of guidance is what gives this conception of education its great and somewhat perilous imaginative appeal, but we are not *compelled* to see them in this way. Still less are we compelled to see education essentially as guidance, or the teacher essentially as a guide. The adoption of this educational Idea, as any other, is a free choice of a particular poetic way of seeing things. Objectively, the choice rests on an analogy which has a certain strength and which saves it from being merely wilful; subjectively, it rests, no doubt, on the imaginative appeal of the Idea.

Near the start of this chapter, I suggested that the metaphors of education lack depth if they are thought without reference to the theories with which they are associated. I went on to suggest that their metaphorical aspect is eliminable, without loss of descriptive capacity. It could be added that no metaphor can give us an insight into the essence of education, for education is not a natural species and does not have an essence. It is incredible, furthermore, that a metaphor should be sufficient in itself to change the current general conception of education. For such a change to be possible there would have had already to have been large-scale intellectual changes, a prodigious shifting of the cultural background, including at least the virtual emergence of a new theory of education with which the metaphor is in deep affinity. A metaphor on its own is no more able to re-structure the cultural background than an eagle out over an abyss is able to re-structure the mountain background. Metaphor is nevertheless of great importance for human beings who, being embodied, have senses, imagination and feeling as conditions of action, and depend upon vitality for the accomplishment of the work of their spirit.

Notes

1. Growth theory is very fully discussed in Dearden (1975). A rather more sympathetic, but still critical, account to which I am also indebted is provided by Darling (1982).
2. Hegel's account of the role of imagination in the formation of general ideas is relevant here. See Wallace and Miller (1971).
3. Hoare and Smith (1971), pp. 34–5, 353; see also Hoare (1977), p. 13, and Entwistle (1979), pp. 41–2.

Chapter Four
The Paradox of Metaphor: A sixteenth-century case study
Kenneth Charlton

As previous chapters have reminded us, educational discourse is littered with metaphors. I have decided, however, to resist the temptation to continue the tradition already established in this collection of sharing with you my favourite mixed metaphors. We should rather, I think, keep our feet firmly on the ground and not sit on the fence; we should take on board the advice of our grass roots colleagues who work at the coalface, and who never get bogged down in airy-fairy theories. They, after all, much prefer to deal with the nuts and bolts of education, even if occasionally they do massage the statistics to suit their case — and if there's a grain of truth in what they say, I know it won't fall on stony ground; at the very least you will take it all with a pinch of salt.

As an historian I'm always interested to follow the way in which some of our metaphorical usage changes (or doesn't change) over the years. As I was preparing this piece I was reminded of a series of pamphlets produced for use in the Army during 1942 and 1943. The series was called *The British Way and Purpose*, and was designed to prepare army personnel for the brave new world which was to be created once Hitler was defeated.

One of the pamphlets was entitled *Education and the Citizen*, jointly authored by E.S. Roberts, formerly headmaster of Devizes Grammar School, and T.R. Weaver 'of the Directorate of Army Education' — later to have an existence in the Institute of Education as Professor Sir Toby Weaver, recently retired from a Deputy Secretaryship in the Department of Education and Science. Like the 1981 DES pamphlet *The School Curriculum*, our joint authors talked about the need for a 'balanced curriculum', and illustrated their views with a small cartoon diagram of a set of scales balanced on a fulcrum labelled 'The School and its Curriculum'. Astride the fulcrum was the figure of 'The Teacher', keeping the balance between at one end of the scale 'The Child and his Needs' and at the other end 'The World and its Activities' (it was of course a *boy*, and in short trousers too, which represented 'The Child'). I wonder whether, if he had still been at the DES in 1981, Sir Toby would have used the same metaphor and so unequivocally given the *controlling* influence over the curriculum to the teacher?

This use of metaphor is on the face of it a puzzling habit for educators in the twentieth century, brainwashed as we are — sorry, I'll withdraw *that* metaphor — *used* as we are to that elaborate metaphor for explaining the physical world called 'scientific method', which amongst other things insists on *plain* language to carry its message — what William Taylor called 'a more accurate and invariant use of terms'. Why, it may be asked, clothe or cloak our discourse with a second layer of puzzling and perhaps misleading terminology, intelligible only to 'insiders', those already acquainted with what Max Black (1962, p. 43) called 'a system of associated commonplaces'? Why abandon our originally simple and direct terminology for a complex and indirect usage?

Paradoxically, of course, we make use of such figurative language in order the better to elucidate complex matters. Not for nothing was the Latin word for metaphor 'translatio', as Erasmus (Knott, 1978) put it, 'so called because a word is transferred away from its real and proper significa-tion to one which lies outside its proper sphere'. The *less* the similarity the *bolder* the metaphor (as we say), the more striking, the more forceful, the more illuminating it is claimed to be — illuminating, that is, to the reader, whose ability to read back from the metaphor to the original in the writer's mind is crucial to the whole operation. It was not only the author but it is now the reader, too, who has to have what Aristotle called in his *Poetics* (21, 1459a), 'an eye for resemblances'. If the similitude of the metaphor is not spotted and understood by the reader then the metaphor fails in its purpose.

I say 'reader' here, but mention of Aristotle should remind us that the reader's predecessor was the listener, that the elucidator, the illuminator, the metaphor-framer was the orator or rhetorician — and this raises two difficulties which can no longer be postponed. The first is that every source of illumination, every attempt at illumination, produces its own shadows; secondly, the term 'rhetoric' is used in the twentieth century almost always in a pejorative sense; 'rhetoric' is almost always 'mere rhetoric', the sort of utterance ('discourse' would be too respectable a word for it), that one hears, for example, at the hustings or in the House of Commons. There are, I believe, still some departments of rhetoric in American universities. The teachers in such departments have their own professional association, The

Speech Association of America, though they changed the original title of their journal from the *Quarterly Journal of Public Speaking* (first published in 1915) to the *Quarterly Journal of Speech* (in 1938) — and I've no doubt that some will argue that they should change it again to, say, *The Quarterly J. of Speech Science.*

This decline in the reputation of rhetoric as a field of study as well as of practice, is of course of longer standing. Traditionally, Thomas Spratt, (1667, p. 113) seventeenth-century historian of the newly-founded Royal Society, is cited — claiming as he did that metaphorical language was 'a trick' which had led inevitably to the 'many mists and uncertainties these specious tropes and figures have brought to our knowledge'. Others cite Bacon, who complained at the beginning of the century in his *Advancement of Learning* that

> men begin to hunt more after words than matter; and more often choiceness of phrase, and the round and clean composition of the sentence, and the sweet falling of the clauses, and the varying and illustration of their works with tropes and figures, than after weight of matter, worth of subject, soundness of argument, life of invention and depth of judgement. (Spedding, Ellis and Heath, 1857, III, p. 284)

Indeed Galileo wished to go even further, insisting that even plain words themselves were not enough. What is needed (he argued) is a totally new language, the language not of words but of numbers. He speaks of the great book of the universe (itself a metaphorical commonplace of his day) which lies forever before our eyes, but which we cannot read, since we have not learned the script in which it was written. 'It is written', he says, 'in a mathematical language, and the characters are triangles, circles and the geometrical figures.' (Quoted Curtius, 1953, p. 324.)

But in fact criticism of rhetoric is to be found back in the Ancient World, and derives from its traditionally two-fold characterization, as (1) the art of embellishment and ornament, and (2) the art of communication and persuasion. On both counts the early rhetoricians were criticized (1) for wasting the time of their pupils by teaching them to use language that was 'merely' ornamental and in the end superfluous, and (2) for so training their pupils in the art of persuasion that a rhetorician who could persuade his audience that black was white was better than his competitor who could not (as Milton's Belial did in *Paradise Lost* (II, 112), 'making the worse appear the better reason').

Of course (as always) what was being criticized was not rhetoric but the *abuse* of rhetoric, and (again as always) there was plenty of that to criticize.

But the great rhetoricians (writers and teachers) of the ancient world — Isocrates, Cicero, Quintilian — each insisted that the rhetorician should be not merely a skilled and persuasive speaker but 'a *good* man skilled in speaking' (*vir bonus dicendi peritus*). They insisted that 'perspicuity (not ornament) was the chief excellence of language', that the object of rhetoric was to 'throw a flood of light on the subject', that the chief end of all of this was to persuade men to do good things.[1] As Cicero put it at the beginning of his *De Inventione*, 'wisdom without eloquence does little good in civic life . . . whilst eloquence without wisdom is generally highly disadvantageous and is never helpful.' This *necessary* relationship between *eloquentia* and *sapientia* remained a crucial element in writings on the subject in medieval Christendom, *par excellence* in Book IV of St. Augustine of Hippo's *De Doctrina Christiana*. We should not be surprised, therefore, that the accepted metaphor for rhetoric was the open palm (as contrasted with the closed fist of dialectic).

With the early fifteenth century in Italy (which saw the re-application of Cicero's views on the value of rhetoric to the civic humanism of Florence) and in the late fifteenth and early sixteenth century in Northern Europe (which saw the re-application of rhetorical skills by Erasmus and his followers to the sphere of biblical and theological scholarships) the place and standing of rhetoric (and therefore of metaphor) come under even closer scrutiny.

In these historical contexts we see metaphor in action in two spheres of education. The first refers to discourse not only about what should go on in school and university, but also in the family with parents as teachers, and in the church with priests as teachers. The second relates to a more technical aspect, to the host of rhetorical manuals written for teachers, undergraduates and pupils. I take the latter first, and then only to *mention* it, since it is not crucially germane to my theme, referring primarily as it does to the *acquisition* of figurative language, and not to the metaphors themselves. These manuals are important in another sense, however, since they would have been studied by any educated man (and some women) in the sixteenth century, who would thus be very well aware of the prescription underlying even the most technical manual, namely that figurative language was to be regarded not only as ornament but as part of any educated person's intellectual equipment.

The metaphors used in the discourse, that is in the literature, of sixteenth-century education relate to every aspect of the matter, and are so all-pervasive that I can mention only a few. In a society that was still predominantly rural, it is not surprising that what, all-embracingly, might be called horticultural metaphors abound. Writing to his friend Niccolò degli Albizzi, the great Italian humanist of the latter part of the fifteenth century, Marsilio Ficino, reminds him that 'The tree of knowledge, even if it seems to have rather bitter roots, nevertheless brings forth the sweetest possible fruit.' (Language Department of the School of Economic Science, 1975) In considering the perennial problem of what and what not to include in the curriculum and why, writers continued to use the metaphor of the bee. James Sandford, for example, justifying his translation of *The Amorous and Tragicall Tales of Plutarch* (1867), reminded his readers that 'the bee gathers honey from the stinking flower and the rose that smelleth sweet' (following Seneca, *Epistolae Morales*, 84, 3–6). It was not for nothing that Lorenzo de' Medici had the books of his library inscribed with the motif of a beehive surrounded by a coronet of bees, or that Richard Foxe, Bishop of Winchester, called his newly-founded (1517) college of Corpus Christi, Oxford, 'this our bee-hive' (the college magazine is to this day entitled *The Beehive*).

Sir Thomas Elyot in his treatise on the education of *The Governour*, justified his inclusion of poetry from the 'lascivious' Ovid and the 'dissolute' Martial by also taking his reader into the garden. It would be more reasonable to deny the study of these poets (he claimed) than it would be

> to forbear or prohibit a man to come into a fair garden lest the redolent savours of sweet herbs and flowers shall move him to wanton courage, or lest, gathering good and wholesome herbs he may happen to be stung by a nettle. No wise man entereth into a garden but he soon espieth good herbs from nettles, and treadeth the nettles under his feet whiles he gathereth good herbs. (ed. Lehmberg, 1962, p. 50)

The teacher in this educational enterprise, whether schoolmaster, parent or cleric, had long been likened to a gardener. He not only tilled the soil, he sowed the seed and tended the growing plant — and 'as plants measurably watered grow the better, but watered too much are drowned and die, so the mind that with moderate labour is refurbished, but with over much is utterly dulled' (Palfreyman, 1567). We find the same metaphor in Francis Bacon's Essay 'Of Nature in Men' where, after that most marvellous example of the rhetorician's art, 'Nature is often hidden, sometimes overcome, seldom extinguished', he goes on to remind us that 'man's nature runs either to herbs or to weeds; therefore let him reasonably water the one and destroy the other' (in Hawkins, 1972, pp. 117–18).

The difficulty lay in achieving agreement as to which parts of man's nature were weed-like and which herb-like. Not surprisingly, after over a thousand years of repetition, the Old Testament-based Christian view of children and childhood persisted, even with the Reformation when the view tended to be reinforced. Lewis Bayley (1612) was in no way unusual when he asked the rhetorical question 'What is youth but an untamed beast?', making more dramatic Edward Hake's (1574, Sig. C3 verso) assertion that 'children are by nature evyll, and being evyll they are by example of parentes made worse'.

The Italian humanists and their Erasmian successors applied their claims about the dignity of man to both teacher and pupil alike, taking more heed the enjoinder of Jesus, 'suffer little children to come unto me'. As Erasmus (trans. Born 1936 p. 140) put it in his *Education of a Christian Prince* (1516),

> hence from the very cradle, as it were, the mind of the future prince, while still open and unmoulded, must be filled with salutary thoughts. Then the seeds of morality must be sown in the virgin soil of his spirit, so that little by little they may grow and mature through age and experience, and remain firmly implanted throughout the course of life. Nothing remains so deeply and tenaciously rooted as those things learned in the first years.

A far cry from the view which assigned to both child and adult a perpetual as well as an innate sinfulness, an innate propensity to do evil rather than good. John Earle (1628, Sig. B2 verso) varied the metaphor, but repeated only part of the Erasmian stance when he likened a child to

> . . . a man in small letter, yet the best copy of Adam before he tasted Eve or the Apple. He is nature's fresh picture newly drawn in oil, where time and much handling dims and defaces. His soul is yet a white paper unscribbled with observations of the world wherewith at length it becomes a blurr'd notebook. He is purely happy because he know no evil, nor hath made means by sin to be acquainted with misery . . . The elder [*sic*] he grows he is a stair lower from God, and like his first father much worse in his breeches.[2]

The humanists developed their theory of childhood from their theory of man, and the fifteenth-century Italians, Vittorino, Guarino and others, implemented their ideas in the relatively peaceful ambience of the court school. Elsewhere the seed did indeed fall on the stony ground of, for example, the public grammar school, where imperfectly educated teachers, trying to cope with a heterogeneous group of variously-motivated pupils, sought refuge in the increasingly influential Calvinist climate, in which the proof-texts (and metaphors) were taken from the Old rather than the New

Testament. Moreover, in so doing, they buttressed their views by citing classical authors on the malleability of the 'green twigs' who appeared before them, at the same time taking comfort in the idea that such malleability would enable the teacher to inhibit the better his pupils' propensities for evil. As Augustine of Hippo had put it long ago in his *Confessions* I:30: 'Is this childish innocence? . . . It is not, Lord, it is not.'

Teachers thus saw themselves in a situation in which there was little room (or even desire) to follow Montaigne's search after a way of producing a child who, having read his 'authors', would 'imbibe their ways of thinking not learn their precepts'. They were not making a merely contingent point when they denied his enjoinder:

> Let the tutor make his charge pass everything through a sieve and lodge nothing in his head on mere authority and trust . . . The bees plunder the flowers here and there, but afterwards they make of them honey, which is all theirs, it is no longer thyme or marjoram. (trans. Frame 1958 p. 111)

Montaigne was, of course, writing about the education of his own class (and in particular of the impending male child of Diane de Foix, Comtesse de Gurson — 'You are too noble-spirited to begin otherwise than with a male'), and would have been the first to acknowledge that his prescriptions could not be generalized to apply to children of other classes.

Horticulture did not, of course, monopolize the field (as we say!). The *tower* of knowledge, with all its implied hierarchies of value-judgement placed on various parts of the curriculum, was invariably illustrated in sixteenth-century books with a small boy holding his horn-book about to enter through the door of grammar at the base, to ascend through the seven liberal arts towards theology, the queen of all the sciences, at the top.[3] Quintilian's digestive metaphor in *Institutio Oratoria* (X. 1, 19),

> let us review and reconsider what we have read, and as we swallow our food well-masticated and almost dissolved, in order that it may be more easily digested, so, too, what we read must not be committed to memory and reserved for imitation in a crude state, but must first be softened and as it were reduced to pulp,

is echoed in the Book of Common Prayer's Collect for the Second Sunday in Advent, in which members of the flock were enjoined to 'read, mark, learn and inwardly digest' the Scriptures. In Bacon's Essay 'Of Studies' (ed. Hawkins, 1972, p. 150) the metaphor is widened to include all books, even though 'some books are to be tasted, others swallowed and some few to be chewed and digested'. The warning, for such it was in Bacon's eyes, was necessary, for the abuse of learning — 'the first distemper of learning' as he called it — could produce the wrong kind of knowledge, which the schoolmen of the late Middle Ages and their successors in the sixteenth century

> did out of no great quantity of matter and infinite agitation of wit, spin out those laborious webs of learning which are extant in their books; . . . a cobweb of learning, admirable for the fineness of its thread and work, but of no substance or profit. (Spedding *et al.*, 1857, pp. 283–6)

In each of these examples of metaphorical usage in discourse about education the author aims to throw additional light on his subject by his transference, by his 'sort-crossing' (as the modern jargon has it), and thus enrich his readers' understanding of the content, method and purpose of, as well as of participators in, the educational process. Yet the very nature of the metaphor, designed as it was to catch the attention of its hearers and readers, inhibited the author from going on to explore not only its strengths but also its weaknesses, or at the very most its unintended consequences. Not least because all of the metaphors I have cited so far relate only to the education of *the few* — I hesitate to use the word 'elite' since it, like 'rhetoric', has now become *the* pejorative term of our society. So I shall refer to the education of 'the few', and I do so in order to move on to look at the education of *the many*, since in the sixteenth century we have also to consider that revolution which we call the Reformation, which had enormous implications for and impact on the education of the many, and which produced yet another paradoxical situation in language use.

Erasmus and his fellow Christian humanists were perfectly well aware of the linguistic problems underlying their efforts to produce new and scholarly editions of the Bible whether in its original languages of Hebrew and Greek or in a new Latin translation, to replace the Vulgate of St. Jerome, laden as it had become with the distorting and misleading accretions of almost a thousand years of Christian use. In these tasks, as in their new commentaries on the Biblical texts, Erasmus and others used the full range of figurative language skills which classical rhetoric offered them.

Luther and his followers, however, had an additional problem on their hands. Recognizing the need for a continuation of work started by Erasmus in order to improve the education of the clergy, they also had to solve the linguistic problems arising from the notion of 'the priesthood of everyman', in which resided the literally awful personal responsibility of every member of the flock for his (and her) religious life, without the traditionally *necessary* mediation of a priest.

Faced with the education of the masses the reformers could no longer rely on the traditional medium of schooling, the Latin language; they had additionally to make more efficient agencies other than the school — the church (through its liturgy and sermon), the family, and the 'godly booke' of instruction, from the Bible and the Catechism to the host of small manuals and treatises written for the edification of the flock. And all of this naturally had to take place through the medium of the vernacular language — in Northern Europe, at least, as yet lacking the developed flexibility and copiousness of Latin.

The vernacular had, of course, two (alleged) advantages. In the first place it could be understood by the illiterate masses; secondly, and perhaps more importantly, its plain simplicity was in accord with the reformers' more general wish to shuffle off the undesired accretions (ecclesiastical, litur-gical, political, economic, theological) of a thousand years or more of Chris-tianity, and in so doing get back to the source (to the pure spring water, *ad fontes*, as the metaphor put it) of the primitive Christian way, enshrined in the life of Jesus and his disciples, themselves plain men of no great education. If the truths of Christianity were to be sought anew, they were to be sought not in the medieval commentators, but in the scriptures them-selves, which would be expounded in the vernacular sermon, delivered in a plain and therefore unrhetorical style.

Of course, all of this was to be found long before Luther appeared on the scene. In late fourteenth-century England, for example, John Wyclif and his followers early recognized the need for a vernacular Bible and for sermons with plain style, if the education of the flock was to be undertaken efficiently (Auski, 1975). But as a medium for the religious (and political) education of the flock neither the Bible nor the sermon was without diffi-culty. It was one thing to assert — and it was repeatedly asserted — that Holy Writ had a single, unified meaning that could be read and understood by all, or that 'There is but one true, proper and genuine sense of Scripture arising from the words rightly understood which we call the literal.'[4]

Such assertions not only got over the pedagogical difficulty of intel-ligibility, but also conveniently denied the Church's traditional insistence that the Bible often implied more than it literally stated, that it could be understood, therefore, only through the identification of several, tradi-tionally four (Caplan, 1929), levels and kinds of meaning, which required careful exegesis by the clergy, who themselves needed the support of the hermeneutical tradition of biblical scholarship (however cleansed by the philological and historical skills of the Erasmians).

But as we know to this day a vernacular Bible (whether Authorized, Revised, Moffat or New English) is far from problem-free, more especially in the matter of its figurative language. Even before the Authorized Version was produced in 1611, the different versions culminating in the Bishops' Bible and the Geneva Bible, could not by their very nature produce a definitive text, free from problems of interpretation. Even the translators of the Geneva Bible, undoubtedly more certain in their faith than most, and expressing that certainty in a multiplicity of metaphors, claiming in their Preface that the Word of God

> . . . is the light to our paths, the keye of the Kingdom of Heaven, our comfort in affliction, our shielde and sworde against Satan, the school of all wisdom, the glass wherein we beholde God's face, the testimony of his favour and the only food and nourishment of our souls,

found it necessary to add a host of marginal glosses to their text in order to clarify the meaning of the message. And not surprisingly, since the traditional interpretations of the metaphors found therein were beginning to appear too simple to an increasingly enquiring flock. Christ's metaphorical likening of his body and blood to the bread and wine of the Last Supper increasingly plagued cleric and layman alike in their efforts to arrive at an understanding of the meaning of that part of the liturgy, the Eucharist, in which they actively participated, and more particularly to arrive at an understanding of the role of the priest in that transaction. In the same way the traditional metaphor which saw the priest as the shepherd of his flock had problems of interpretation and understanding for both priesthood and laity, especially when some of the laity (and indeed some of the clergy) pondered on the nature and habits of sheep, to say nothing of the wolves who invariably made their appearance when the shepherd metaphor was used. The translator of Heinrich Bullinger's *Decades* (ed. Harding, 1849), a collection of fifty sermons, makes elaborate use of the metaphor. In so doing, however, he unconsciously reveals the difficulties and deserves extensive quotation:

> Now the sheep, whereof spiritual shepherds have undertaken charge, are not beasts, but men: the very images of God himself endued with ever-living souls, citizens with saints and blessed angels, clothed with God's livery, beautified with his cognizance and all the badges of salvation, admitted to his table, and to no meaner dishes than the body and blood of the undefiled Lamb, Jesus Christ; bought also and redeemed out of the wolf's clawes with no less price than of that same blood, more precious than any gold or silver. Sheep also of that nature they are, that, being carefully fed and discreetly ordered they prove gentle and loving towards their shepherds, and serviceable towards the chief Shepherd Jesus Christ; but being neglected and left to themselves they degenerate into bloody wolves, watching every opportunity when they may rent in pieces their shep-

herds and all other sheep which are not degenerated into their wolfish nature . . .
No remedy, then, but the ministry of this time must forthwith, without further
delay set themselves to feed their flocks, to teach, to exhort, to strengthen, to
bind up, to build, to plant, to water, to set, to graft, to leave nothing undone that
appertaineth to the feeding and fatting of the Lord's flocks, to the planting of the
Lord's paradise, tilling of the Lord's husbandry, dressing of the Lord's vine-
yard, raising and rearing up of the Lord's temple. (Translator's Preface)

Even when the metaphor was varied, the educative function of the priest
remained the same:

As the little birds perke up their heads when the dame cometh with the meate
. . . so you are here like birds, and we the dame and the word the food. Therefore
you must prepare a mouth to take it. (*Sermons of Master Henry Smith*, 1601,
p. 302)

The ABC of the Christian is to learn the arte of Learning; we care how we sow
lest our seed be lost, so let us care how we learne, lest God's seede be lost. There
is no seede which groweth so fast as the Lord's seede, if it be sown well. (Ibid.,
p. 300)

The problem of the simple and the true has perennially plagued cleric
and lay teachers alike. Elizabeth I might well claim — in her much-quoted
metaphor — that she had no wish to 'make a window into men's souls'. But
she was acutely aware that the problem of control in the religious education
of her subjects was inextricably bound up with their political education. At
her accession she issued a proclamation forbidding all preaching 'until
consultation may be had with Parliament'. Subsequently she persisted with
the policy of controlling her clergy, not only by keeping a close watch on the
universities where they were educated, but also by issuing licences to
preach only to the orthodox and by insisting that those not licensed should
read the Homilies 'for the better service of Almighty God and the quietness
of this realm'. She even saw household instruction as dangerous, and noted
with irritation that

every merchant must have his schoolmaster and nightly conventicles,
expounding scripture and catechizing their servants and maids, insomuch that I
have learned how some maids have not sticked to control learned preachers and
say 'such a man taught otherwise in our house' (Neale, 1973, p. 314).

'Gadding to sermons' came to be seen as an offence. James I complained
of 'itching tongues' and banned the afternoon service and its sermon.
Charles I was merely acknowledging what was usual when he remarked
that 'people are governed by pulpits more than by the sword in times of
peace' (Gardiner, 1898, III p. 135).

Even so, this does not tell the whole story, for there were at the same time plenty of writers and teachers in the sixteenth century who persisted in their claim that the classical view of rhetoric was valid. The many critics of rhetoric were, as I have said, criticizing an *abuse* of rhetoric. Erasmus ambiguously entitled his own criticism of the abuse *Ciceronianus* (1529), for at the beginning of the sixteenth century the term 'Ciceronian' (as with 'Leavisite' in our day) had both pejorative and honorific connotations. But properly used (he claimed on another occasion; Mynors, 1978, pp. 130–131) the value of metaphor was infinite:

> Do you wish to entertain? Nothing adds more sparkle. Are you concerned to convey information? Nothing else makes your point so convincingly, so clearly. Do you intend to persuade? Nothing gives you greater penetration. Have you a mind to expatiate? Nowhere is plenty readier to your hand. Or to be brief? Nothing leaves more to the understanding . . .

Roger Ascham, (ed. Giles, 1864, III, p. 211), in his search for both 'good matter and good utterance' went further even than Cicero himself in claiming that the quality of a society's language was but a reflection of the quality of that society's moral life. The same point was argued in those 'Apologies' for and 'Defences' of poetry which appeared towards the end of the sixteenth and on into the seventeenth century, in which it was claimed that a closer apprehension of truth was to be found in metaphor-laden 'creative fiction' (as we would now call it) than in any other form. Though he was highly critical of 'a foolish and affected eloquence' in the fictive writer, Ben Jonson was adamant nonetheless that 'we do not require in him mere Elocution' — the ultimate form of abuse to this day being to equate rhetoric with elocution — 'nor simply an excellent facility in verse; but an exact knowledge of all virtues and their contraries, with ability to render the one loved and the other hated by his proper embattling them' (ed. Herford *et al.*, 1945, p. 595). The task of the poet, claimed Sir Philip Sidney, was

> both to delight and to teach; and delight to move men to take that goodness in hand which without delight they would fly as from a stranger, and teach to make them to know that goodness whereunto they are. (ed. Smith, 1904, I, p. 158)

In his *Tractate* Milton (ed. Patterson, 1931–40) criticized that classroom abuse of rhetoric which led children to learn 'meer words' and

> forced [their] empty wits . . . to compose theams, verses and orations, which are the acts of ripest judgement and the final work of a head filled by long reading and observing with elegant maxims and copious inventions. These are not matters to be wrung out of poor striplings like blood out of a nose or the plucking of untimely fruit. (*Works*, IV, p. 278)

For, as he noted on another occasion

> . . . in the orator as in the poet nothing commonplace or mediocre can be allowed
> . . . he who wishes deservedly to be and be considered an orator ought to be
> equipped and perfected with a certain and encompassing support of all the arts
> and all the sciences . . . True eloquence, therefore, I find to be none but the
> serious and hearty love of truth. (*Works*, XII, pp. 247–9)

George Chapman (1595) who as much as many in his day sought to
develop and make use of the rhetorical potentialities of the vernacular
tongue, insisted that

> . . . obscurity in affection of words and undigested conceits is pedanticall and
> childish; but where it shroudeth itself in the hart of his subject, uttered with
> fitnes of figures and expressive epithets, with that darknes wil I still labour to be
> shadowed; rich minerals are digged out of the bowels of the earth, not found in
> the superficies and dust of it.

In an age — our own, I mean — when we are constantly being urged to
acknowledge the superiority of science and its 'plain' means of communication, I would want to press, on the contrary, for *more* metaphor, with its
helpful as well as its difficult ambiguities, to remind us that life, and
therefore education, is more accurately and realistically described by words
such as paradox and ambiguity than by words such as pure and simple. As
Oscar Wilde reminded us in Act 1 of *The Importance of Being Earnest*, 'The
truth is rarely pure and never simple; and life would be very tedious if it
were.'

It is precisely because our pupils, relatively inexperienced in the use of
language, insist on taking our words literally that those misunderstandings
called 'howlers' occur. They might amuse us for a while, until we ponder
on the gross failure of our attempts to communicate. As communicators
teachers are perennially faced with the problem of reconciling the simple
and the true — how to clarify the truth for others (children and adults) who
both need (intellectually) and prefer (emotionally) the simple.

Being an *undeclared* analogy, the metaphor postulates not merely a like-
ness but also an identity, and in this lies both its strength and its danger, too
easily and too often leading us to mistake the mask for the face, to confuse a
special view of the world with the world itself. We need, therefore, to take
what William Taylor called 'epistemological precautions' — not by using
the prophylactic sheath called for by Harold Entwistle (1970, p. 156), who
wishes 'to dispense with metaphors altogether', but by acknowledging the

complexity of language and its contexts, and by using it, whether in academic discourse or in the schoolroom, with a due awareness of its rich and enriching complexity. As Erasmus himself said, long ago,

> you may observe that none are more given to constant quibblings over the minutiae of language than those who boast that they pass over mere words and concentrate on the matter itself (ed. MacGregor, 1978, p. 666)

And with that I'll stop, encouraged to do so by the thought that (in Bacon's metaphor) 'Silence is the sleep which nourisheth wisdom.'

Notes

1. Quintilian, *Institutio Oratoria*, XII. 1, 1; V. 14, 34; and cf. VIII. 2, 22–4.
2. Cf. Erasmus, *De Pueris Instituendis*, 1529: 'Handle the wax while it is soft, mould the clay while it is moist, dye the fleece before it is stained.' (In Woodward, 1964, p. 187).
3. Cf. Gregorius Reisch, *Margarita Philosophica*, 1503.
4. Whitaker (trans. Fitzgerald, 1849). Cf. Cannon, 1962, pp. 129–38.

Chapter Five
The Role of Metaphor in Psychological Research
Liam Hudson

When I first learnt to be a psychologist, a quarter of a century ago in Oxford, metaphors were seen as peripheral to our endeavours; a form of playfulness. In retrospect, though, they seem to have dominated us to a disconcerting degree. In terms of philosophical assumption, we were all navvies, patiently adding one brick after another to the great house of knowledge. The truthfulness of each brick was certified, we assumed, by the scientific method that we had been taught to practise. Progress might at times seem slow, but it was inexorable.

Within that system of belief, itself metaphorical, we seized on metaphors that were more specific. The brain was viewed as a telephone exchange; or, alternatively, man was assumed to be a rat. There was excitement in the air; the sense that these analogies were discoveries, and that the key to the understanding of the central nervous system might now be in our hands.

All that seems long ago; an age of pioneering and of naïvety, of categorical exclusions as crude as they were unwitting. Ordinary language, it is worth noting, we ignored almost in its entirety; a strange omission in a city dominated by philosophers committed to the study of ordinary language. When we admitted language, we did so, I remember, with an air of primness, as 'vocalization'.

Slowly, the climate in which I worked changed. At Cambridge, when I had finished my Ph D and was starting to research in earnest, I felt around me for the first time the presence of sociological, and more specifically anthropological, modes of thought. Dimly, it dawned on me that the mind might be organized not like a mechanism but like a culture. Initially, though, none of this mattered. My own research was lodged within the conventions, the mind-set, of mental measurement, and for that reason I did not have to think about the mind at all. Rather, I dealt with externals. I found it natural, for example, to conceive of the careers I was studying as progress up ladders, or as races across hurdles.

There were absurd-seeming consequences. Success at one level of the educational system often correlated only poorly, I found, with success at another level. Brilliantly successful schoolboys often got poor degrees. A surprisingly large number of brilliantly successful scientists, Fellows of the Royal Society, had mediocre academic records behind them; likewise High Court Judges and Cabinet Ministers. Shock and horror would have dissolved in a moment had I and my audience been more careful in our use of metaphor. Instead of ladders or hurdles, we could have imagined a movement across thresholds from field to field, or from room to room, in which the requirements placed on the individual might be as dissimilar as those imposed on us by kitchen and dining room, bathroom and bedroom. Those who wash thoroughly do not necessarily sleep well; those who enjoy their food are often inadequate cooks. Competence in one venue, in other words, may have little bearing on competence in another.

Intellectually, my progress in research in those formative years seems in retrospect to have consisted very largely in fighting my way clear of inappropriate systems of metaphor — without realizing that this was what I was doing. The problem of pigeon-holes illustrates this. It was convenient, I discovered, to divide members of a population, students say, into contrasting groups: 'convergers', in my terms, as opposed to 'divergers' (Hudson, 1968). This artifice was useful to me at the time, and remained useful — for example in the work on sleep and dream recall done in the Edinburgh sleep laboratory in the 1970s. Unfortunately, it is also the perfect vehicle for a simple-minded assumption about 'types': the belief that people can sensibly be placed in one or other psychological pigeon-hole. Slowly and quite painfully, I have had to struggle clear of this preoccupation with 'types' to the notion that I now hold: that we each strike a balance, in terms of our intellectual functioning, between opposed fears — the fear, on the one hand, of making a mistake, and the fear on the other of being intellectually circumscribed or trapped. From thinking, always uneasily, about types, I have moved on to thinking in terms of systems that embody irreconcilable tension or ambivalence; to my mind, a step in the right direction.

An equally arbitrary metaphor had imposed itself on our processes of data analysis. We correlated and chi-squared in those days because we knew no better; but those who did know better were guided by the metaphors of agriculture. Men like Fisher assumed that causes in psychology were additive and continuous in their action, like fertilisers on crops of corn. We have since learnt from Zeeman that quite different patterns of action are mathematically acceptable: the steps and lurches of catastrophe theory. We have also discovered what we could perfectly well have guessed: that causes can interact according to logically complex patterns, arranging themselves in sequences, or as alternatives, even showing reversals — a state of affairs that Tanner's (1978) recent studies of physical growth display well.

By the time I had reached Edinburgh, in the late 1960s, this agricultural metaphor had been prised loose from its bed of apparently God-given mathematical procedure, and was labelled, somewhat derisively, as 'agricultural botany', or 'agric. bot.' for short. This orthodox but artificial view of research was contrasted with the notion of 'illuminative evaluation' brought to Edinburgh from MIT by Malcolm Parlett (Parlett and Hamilton, 1976). Institutions, like people, are complexes of meaning, it was realized; and it was part of the psychologist's task to explicate these — to open them out, to make them plain. In a word, to *illuminate* them; and do so for the benefit of those most immediately concerned.

Although we were shaking ourselves free from certain patently maladaptive metaphors, arbitrary or even positively obstructive in their effects, we were still not free to tell ourselves what we were doing. Oddly, metaphor remained a taboo topic. While still in Cambridge, I had tried to talk about the role of metaphors in psychological research — at the Institute of Education, as it happens — but had felt guilty, as though I were engaged in some arty species of cheat. And even when I reached Edinburgh, which at the time was a great bastion of excellence in linguistics, the topic of metaphor remained awkward. I raised it on several occasions, in the setting, for example, of the School of Epistemics, but provoked embarrassment and let the matter slide. (At the time, metaphors were assumed, I think, to be messy and vague, and at odds with the twin ruling preoccupations: to analyse out the deep structure of language and to marry such linguistic analysis to the language of computers.)

Help has come more recently in the form of two books. As usual, I learnt what I needed to learn by being asked to review them. The first is William Gass's remarkable text, *On Being Blue* (1976). A philosopher and experimental novelist, Gass's concern is with the problem of how the poet or novelist renders his sentences sexual; how he contrives to fill his sentences with meanings that are erotic. This is not primarily a matter of referring to sexual acts, nor of using dirty words. Nor is it just a matter of exploiting the formal properties of words. It is at root a matter of metaphor: of fashioning 'containers of consciousness' that the author can freight with the appropriately elusive meanings. The task is not simple, Gass reminds us:

> It is not simple, not a matter for amateurs, making sentences sexual; it is not easy to structure the consciousness of the reader with the real thing, to use one wonder to speak of another, until in the place of the voyeur who reads we have fashioned the reader who sings; but the secret lies in seeing sentences as containers of consciousness, as constructions whose purpose it is to create conceptual perceptions — blue in every area and range: emotion moving through the space of the imagination, the mind at gleeful hop and scotch, qualities, through the arrangement of relations, which seem alive within the limits they pale and redden like spanked cheeks, and thus the bodies, objects, happenings, they essentially define. (p. 86)

It is skill, what is more, that alienates the author from what he describes:

> So to the wretched writer I should like to say that there's one body only whose request for your caresses is not vulgar, is not unchaste, untoward, or impolite: the body of your work itself; for you must remember that your attentions will not merely celebrate a beauty but create one; that yours is love that brings its own birth with it, just as Plato has declared, and that you should therefore give up the blue things of this world in favor of the words which say them. (p. 89)

Put prosaically, the fashioning of poetic sentences is a little like planning a garden or creating a scheme of interior decoration: a question of directing the reader's gaze, without crudely determining it; of setting up systems of resonance and echo that are orderly, yet are in principle open-ended, indeterminate.

The special interest of Gass's text is that it is, itself, brilliantly elusive. He offers you the prospect of lists, the possibility of taxonomy, even of an explanatory manual, but you never get these, or, more strictly, never know whether you have got them or not. The vision of lists melting into evocative prose is certainly a potent metaphor of sexual experience; but it still leaves scope for an approach that is more plodding. It is just this that the second text, Lakoff and Johnson's *Metaphors We Live By* (1980), provides.

Lakoff and Johnson give lists and examples in full abundance, and they establish beyond all reasonable doubt that our ordinary language is saturated with metaphor, through and through; that you cannot put together a sentence with which to discuss ideas without using metaphors to help you on your way. Typically, our ideas about ideas are grounded, they claim, in terms of our ideas about the physical. And this dependence of one sort of idea upon another is no more mysterious, in principle, than is syntax. We can discuss meanings just as we can discuss grammar.

Their first example stakes out the ground. They point out that we conceive of argument as war. The language of argument is, at root, the language of physical combat. But they also point out that it need not be so: that one can easily imagine societies in which argument is conceived differently — for example, as theatrical performance. In such a society, both argument itself and the criteria for success or failure in argument would be quite unlike our own.

Metaphors, in other words, are not idle flourishes. They shape what we do. Lakoff and Johnson go on to discuss the extent to which we think of theories as though they were buildings, falling naturally to talk of foundations, bases, structures, frameworks, etc. Administrations, they observe, are entities we habitually think of spatially, in terms of up and down. (When we move into positions of authority, we conceive of ourselves moving up, not across, certainly not down.) Endlessly, it seems, we are doomed to make play, as I have in the last sentence, with the categories of up and down, in and out. Henry may be in the kitchen; he may be in the Army; he may be in love.

Between them, Gass's book and Lakoff and Johnson's came as a great relief. They set me free to talk about the difficulties that metaphors in psychology present. But what is one to do? Is it realistic to imagine psychology purged of metaphor, at least to the extent that physics now is? The correct path, I believe, is not to attempt any such purge. Rather, to accept our metaphors; to colonize them, and make their formal properties explicit.

This policy is not easy, however, because the setting in which we pursue it is changing. As Clifford Geertz (1980, p. 165) has recently pointed out, the various genres of academic life are showing every sign of blurring one into the other. While still bounded by arbitrary conventions, these genres and disciplines defined no-man's-lands. Now the exploration of these no-man's-lands has begun. They, too, are permeated with metaphor.

As illustrative of the complex equations of doubt and surprise that such exploratory ventures are likely to face, let me describe, briefly, three recent projects of my own. In each, I have disregarded boundaries of genre, but have remained loyal to those concerns that seem to me genuinely 'psychological' — that make one a psychologist rather than a biologist, say, or a poet, or a painter.

The first of these excursions took the form of a book, *The Nympholepts* (1978). I wrote this in first draft, 70,000 words in a month, with an unparalleled sense of release. Like other psychologists who have written fiction, I was delighted to discover that I was free to be precise; to say what I really thought rather than entering into the mare's nest of caveats, reservations and approximations that utterance as a professional psychologist seems to require.

At one level it is a story about a car crash in which two people, who should not have been together, are accidentally killed; and about the reverberations of that crash on those who survive them. At another, it is an examination of personal need: of the need, more specifically, for certainty in knowledge of those with whom we live intimately — a kind a knowledge that, in principle, we cannot have. ('Nympholepts' are creatures who crave the unattainable, in whatever form.) At yet another level, the text takes the form of a slightly prurient reconstruction, through the eyes of the narrator, of what those two people might have been doing together in that car before it crashed. At this level, it becomes an exercise in the scrutiny of evidence; of the traces that each of us leaves behind, and of what these traces can properly be construed to mean.

The text fails as a novel because it lacks a strong story-line, and it lacks vivid characterization. On the other hand, in its own bleak and modest terms, it still seems to me to work quite well. The use of fiction to explore fact is a time-honoured enterprise, and there are many legitimating precedents for the kind of text I attempted, some of which are recognizable as fiction, while others, more flatly analytic, could pass muster as psychology. Mary McCarthy's autobiographical novel *The Company She Keeps* (1957) is an outstanding example of the first; Doris Lessing's atypical *Not A Very Nice Story* (1972) an instance of the second. Each is 'truthful', it seems to me, managing to say something about people and how they live that has not been matched in non-fiction. Norman Mailer's (1974) biography of Marilyn Monroe occupies an adjacent but separate niche: an imaginative recreation of a life, and in that sense a novel — but, as he says, 'a species of novel ready to play by the rules of biography'; one that reaches through uncertainties towards what actually occurred.

There are bafflements, even so. The most important in my own case concerns the question of parody. The plot of *The Nympholepts*, inasmuch as it exists, is a parody of a whodunit. More worrying, because inadvertent, is the fact that the voice of the narrator is also a parody, an impersonation. While some of the characters are vividly alive to me, six years after I first started to write about them — more real in two cases than almost anyone I know in 'real life' — the narrator is a visitor, an alien. An uncommitted, slightly unpleasant figure, he seems to stand for the voyeurism of psychology; our tendency to pry into the lives of others, rather than living wholeheartedly for ourselves. He is an *empty* man; the embodiment, perhaps, of the emptiness that lies at the heart of empiricism itself.

More recently, I have been writing with enthusiasm about the image of the body in works of art: paintings, sculptures, photography. The book is called *Bodies of Knowledge* (1982), and is an attempt to take seriously the world of visual signs that artists and photographers create; and to do so not as a source of undifferentiated pleasure, a transient 'buzz', but as the equivalent of Gass's poetic sentence: as containers of consciousness that are freighted with all the ambivalences that the human body inspires.

I have written, I believe, as a professional psychologist rather than as an amateur critic or even more amateur historian. And I have done my best to be orderly, not just about certain images like Titian's *Venus and the Organ Player*, for example, and Manet's *Olympia*, but, more generally, about the curious network of relationships between artist, model, image and spectator that springs into being whenever any one of us is moved to point a paint brush or camera at someone we find desirable (or, for that matter, frightening).

Despite its pleasures, this project, like *The Nympholepts*, has about it something worrying. Page after page is devoted to unpacking the layers of meaning that certain images contain. In the course of unpacking these images, I have learnt for the first time actually to 'see' them: to explore them, rather than simply to recognize them and register either approval or disapproval. My own pleasure has grown with each step in the unpacking, each new discovery of a previously buried implication. But, to the reader, I am afraid it must all seem a shade tiresome: I have turned into a species of removals man, expert in packing and unpacking freight from other people's containers. I could get over this obstacle by exploiting the usual expository tricks: jokes, a show of gusto, or adherence, perhaps, to some simple but attractive doctrine that lies outside my subject-matter — a Marxist view of the nude, say. Such tricks are alienating, though, and it seems a shame to fall back on their use.

My third project consists in teaching myself to use a camera, a mode of inquiry closer to psychology than at first sight it seems. (Both are representational activities; both are immersed in issues of technique. Both centre uneasily, as any form of representation must, around John Ruskin's doctrine of 'truth to nature'.) Here, the sources of alienation are obvious. As Susan Sontag (1979) has stressed, and John Berger too, photography constitutes a dislocation of experience, especially intimate experience, of which we should all beware.

With photography it is the advantages rather than the snags that are hidden. In my own efforts I notice, for example, that certain psychologically significant metaphors recur: fields, paths, thresholds, defensive barriers abound. And what is conceptually appealing about these images is their particularity. Idly, we assume that metaphors are *vague*. But in photography, this is not so. A field is not just a field. It is a specific field, with identifiable formal properties. It may stand empty, or have occupants (cows, say). These occupants may have one purpose or different purposes. Neighbouring fields may have similar or quite different occupants (more cows, or horses, or humans in caravans). The threshold, in the form of the gate, may stand open or shut. There may be several thresholds, or only one. The boundaries may be fixed and impenetrably dense, or they may be notional (a single electrified wire, say, as opposed to an old hedgerow). And so on. I labour the point because in psychology, we have grown timid about the detailed relation of evidence to explanation — either gesturing towards our theories with a sweep of the hand, or losing ourselves inside our theories entirely. We can easily be more precise, photography suggests; and it is important that we should be so, because it is in its detail and nuance that the dialectical dance between theory and evidence acquires whatever value it possesses.

Despite the aridity of much of what happens inside the conventional bounds of psychology, and despite the perplexities that await those who venture to blur such bounds, psychology seems at the moment to be in an unusually interesting condition. It is extraordinary in its catholicity. It encompasses a polyglot array of specialists who could pass muster, variously, as biologists, geneticists, computer scientists, philosophers or sociologists. And it remains poised between the sciences and the arts, yet seems reducible to neither. The position is of special interest because, for the first time in decades, the deeper stresses and strains that underlie the systematic study of people are making themselves felt.

The chief of these lies in the fact that, while dedicated to rationality and order, the psychologist faces a subject-matter that is inherently subtle. Both within each head and between heads, ambiguity, ambivalence, inconsistency and conflict are the norm. Far from being ruckles in life's great carpet to be smoothed away, they are stubbornly and irreducibly *there*. The danger, if we over-simplify, is not just that we will make slow progress, but that we will restrict our inquiries to those facets of human experience that are themselves simple. An excessively tidy or reductive psychology could distort those events it is supposed to explain.

As we reflect on psychology rather than practise it, metaphors still hold us in thrall. We end up, as often as not, their captives. One of the most memorable episodes of a chequered career is that of being closeted with a great and gifted philosopher of science, and being shouted at for two hours. His indignation centred on my claim, spelt out in a book, *The Cult of the Fact* (1972), that psychologists would be wise to think about their research as well as doing it. His own position is based on the metaphor of revolutionary politics; of an oscillation between states of normal growth and of radical upheaval. From an individual research worker's point of view the movement from one state of orderly calm to another is a matter of chance. 'You luck it out,' he informed me with force. There is no good and every harm, he seemed to feel, in thinking about research: you get on with it, and leave it to history to decide whether you have been lucky or not.

I still think he was wrong and that I was right. A quasi-religious adherence to a particular metaphor, or family of metaphors, is enough to make you famous, but it is not enough. Psychologists are wise to worry about their own assumptions: not wringing their hands, nor lapsing into enervating states of *angst*, but reflecting systematically, empirically, on the metaphors, models and assumptions they employ. Michel Butor (1971) has described the novel as the 'laboratory of narrative'. By analogy, I see no reason why psychology and the social sciences should not serve as a 'laboratory of metaphor'; one in which we test and taxonomize, becoming knowledgeable about the points where metaphors and models, theories and heuristic devices, fuse. Rather than living unwittingly, unreflectively, in the grip of certain metaphors, we could learn to pick and choose.

Such self-consciousness may make the heart sink; a prospect of psychologists abandoning inquiry into people and what makes them tick, and retreating, instead, into a discipline adjacent to philosophy. This is not my intention at all. We should be more eager to discover what moves people to think and act as they do, not less. But if, to take an example at random, we address a faulty marriage as though we were addressing an internal combustion engine, or a faultily programmed computer, we should be alert to the fact that other metaphors are available. It may be that all available metaphors will fail; that they are at odds with the evidence that stares us in the face. One faulty marriage may prove to resemble nothing so much in the world as another faulty marriage. But in making this discovery, we end not in frustration, but with a set of formal properties that we can use as raw materials in building some new model of our own.

When that happens, one small corner of psychology will start to look very much like a science: an exciting transition to perceive. But whether such a movement from quasi-science to real science will actually occur must remain for the time being in doubt. It may well prove, in each age, that there is one dominant metaphor we fail to identify; and that, as a result, we see ourselves at any one moment as making ratchet-like progress, but find in retrospect that, once again, we have lost our way inside yet another system of metaphor.

Adjacent to this last doubt is uncertainly about what discovery in psychology amounts to. To resort once again to metaphor, there is a sense in which psychological discovery is 'archaeological', a rendering of the implicit explicit. (Tacitly, we all know the rules of English, otherwise we could not speak it; but the explanation of those rules nonetheless constitutes a discovery.) But there is also a sense in which the psychologist, like the biologist or physicist, can hope to build anew: to construct an edifice of theory that predicts what people will say or do.

The first of these alternatives is often assumed to fall within the sphere of hermeneutics, the interpretation of 'texts'; the second within that of science. The first is thought to be a matter of illumination, the second one of control. The first is taken to be friendly; the second to be clinically elegant and cold. My own impression is that this simple polarization — one, roughly, between the 'soft' and the 'hard' — is itself a metaphor or myth, the most pervasive of our time; and that it breaks down whenever one attempts to apply it. There is, after all, impersonal discipline in any art worth pursuing, just as there is irreducible doubt about what happens inside the atom.

There is no question, though, that, sentimentally speaking, these 'soft' and 'hard' options exert attractions that are dissimilar. Personally, I find myself drawn irresistibly towards the prospect of elegance; but know sneakingly, too, that should elegance ever be achieved, I would want to be elsewhere. Is this a damaging admission? I do not think so. The prospect of elegance remains alluring as long as one is in a muddle. But the thought of a world given over entirely to elegance is at least as unattractive as one in which confusion is sovereign. It is unresolved tension that lends these extremes their fascination. And as psychology's underlying tensions are unlikely to resolve themselves of their own accord, a certain degree of ambivalence may well be our lot, not just for the foreseeable future, but for as long as we feel moved to study one another in an orderly way.

Of their own accord, ambivalences bring mixed metaphors in tow. In discussing the puzzles that psychology now embodies, I realize that I have mixed by own metaphors royally. I have invoked fields and foundations, bodies and visions, conflict and cleanliness, and a great deal else besides. Normally bad manners though it is, I have found the mixture appropriate, even comforting. If my nerve had not failed me, I would have committed

much worse excesses. In our choice of metaphors we reveal our invest-
ments, and mine with regard to psychology are nothing if not divided. A
great man for 'coal-faces' and conscientiousness, work for me is manual
work. But in talking of explanation itself, I am drawn towards 'illumination', rather than its counterpart, 'control'. Perhaps there is inconsistency
here; even evidence of a bifurcated nature. But bifurcations are not necessarily maladaptive. On the contrary, they may be just the quirks of
character that the professional study of people demands.

Chapter Six
Metaphor and the Curriculum
Denis Lawton

The first point to be made, despite the fact that it is perhaps painfully obvious, is that the word 'curriculum' is itself a metaphor — 'a course to be run'. It may also be one of those metaphors David Aspin referred to as almost ceasing to be metaphor because the secondary meaning is now more familiar than the Latin primary meaning. When we use the word 'curriculum' now it is most unlikely that we are thinking in *any* way about its original meaning.

It may or may not be significant that we use a metaphorical word for this purpose in English where other languages, for example French, do not. Does it mean that we see curriculum differently? Do they lack a concept because they lack the word? I was tempted to go a little way along this Sapir-Whorf path, but decided against it. My previous excursions into that territory have been almost totally inconclusive, and I doubt whether there is much mileage in this one.

The second point is that curriculum discourse is shot through with metaphors: 'core curriculum', 'spiral curriculum', 'streaming', 'setting' and 'banding', all feature in everyday speech and are controversial issues. But there are not many jokes about curriculum. This is perhaps puzzling: metaphor is closely connected with joking, but not in the curriculum area. Why not?

This was another possible line of attack which I rejected, despite the interesting parallel — jokes are meant to make us laugh, metaphors when used deliberately are often intended to illuminate or enhance understanding. But some jokes do not amuse — who was it who said 'a German joke is no laughing matter'? — and many metaphors confuse rather than clarify. I have to return to that point later.

Another tempting approach was to try to classify curricular metaphors and to see what light that threw either on curriculum or on metaphor. Perhaps even using the categories, or some of them, suggested by Lakoff and Johnson (1980) in *Metaphors We Live By*. This is an interesting approach, but I suspect in the long run not very illuminating. It would be possible to look at, for example:

(a) a curriculum as a building operation — hence *Framework for the School Curriculum* (DES, 1980);

(b) as food — hence balanced diet;

(c) as a plant — hence the core of the curriculum (and presumably the pips and the hard skin);

(d) as a product — Charity James (1968) used to speak of curriculum-making;

(e) as a commodity — hence talk of curriculum packages or even Paolo Freire's (1971) banking metaphor.

It might have been interesting to see what kind of teachers use what kind of metaphors. There might be significant differences in teaching style and practice?

I rejected that approach for two reasons: first, it would require a good deal of empirical research which I do not think anyone has yet attempted, and for which I certainly did not have time to try. Second, because I suspect — for reasons which Professor Aspin outlined — that in most cases there would be no correlation between use of metaphor and classroom practice. Many of the metaphors are so deeply embedded (like the word curriculum itself) in educational language, or even in everyday speech, that they are used automatically rather than consciously. But there may be some important exceptions to that, as I will suggest later.

If anyone does want to make the attempt to engage in the necessary empirical work, I think they should employ another kind of classification as well as the Lakoff and Johnson categories and attempt to say, for example, whether any curriculum metaphor would tend to be *(a)* radical (encouraging change); *(b)* conservative (encouraging stability), or *(c)* reactionary (looking back to a golden age).

An example of the 'radical' might be the *sabre-tooth tiger fable* which rejects the traditional curriculum out of hand (Benjamin, 1971). I suppose the *curriculum as building* metaphor might be an example of 'status quo' — certainly the DES document *Framework for the School Curriculum* (1980) was not radical, neither did it encourage us to look back to better days. We do not have to look far for a 'reactionary' metaphor: *standards*. Barry MacDonald (1978) uses a quotation from Alan Bennett's play *Forty Years On*:

'But don't you think, headmaster, that your standards are out of date?'
'Of course, they are! They would not be standards otherwise.'

That might, incidentally, be an example of a good joke which, like some metaphors, encourages us to evade rather than face a real problem. There might, therefore, be some fruitful outcome from looking at curriculum metaphors in terms not only like those suggested by Lakoff and Johnson (1980), but also cross-classified as 'radical', 'status quo' or 'reactionary'. I hope one day someone else will be tempted to do the necessary empirical work.

Enough about possible approaches which I have decided not to attempt. I should now like to look at three related and overlapping issues: first, curriculum metaphors which might tend to mislead rather than clarify; second, curriculum metaphors which are wrong, perhaps dangerously wrong; and, third, curriculum metaphors which are ideologies in disguise, and which might influence practice.

I said earlier that one possible, intentional, use of metaphor (bearing in mind David Aspin's chapter) was metaphor as clarification. This is a well-known teaching device: we start with something familiar to the student and point out a similiarity in something unknown or less familiar. 'The heart is (like) a pump . . .'; 'the sun is like a big ball of fire . . .'. Helpful, perhaps, at some stage in learning, but not really true!

The interesting question, from a pedagogic point of view, with all such usages is at what point does the simile or metaphor cease to be helpful and begin to be misleading? At what point do we reject the over-simplified model and say reality is much more complicated than *that?*

An example from outside education is remote enough to make the point in an uncontroversial way. Christopher Hill (1967) describes how in the seventeenth century scientific thinking developed dramatically and gave men a new confidence. 'Nature came to be thought of as a machine to be understood, controlled and improved upon by knowledge.' Nature as a machine: Hill suggests that not only was this a tremendously exciting idea, but one which was *liberating;* man was freed from providence or divine will and could not only understand the world better, but could begin to change it. The idea was not confined, of course, to the physical universe, but also to what we now refer to as the world-view of the social sciences. Hill points out that as early as 1549 Sir Thomas Smith had used the analogy of the clock to explain economic causation.

Mechanical analogies soon came to dominate discussions of society and the state as against the traditional organic image of 'the body politic'. With them came the idea that governments might have a positive role to play in exerting man's control over things. (Hill, 1967, p. 207)

Here was a metaphor which was tremendously illuminating and encouraged the development of science and social science thinking. But it was, of course, wrong. The universe is not a machine and if we think of it in that way today, it actually hinders our scientific understanding; similarly, if we continue to think of society as a clock or any other kind of machine, we get stuck at the naïve level of a functionalist world where human beings are cogs in the machine without any of the freedom that scientists and social scientists in the seventeenth century found so exciting.

So when does a metaphor cease to illuminate and begin to confuse? Some answers to that question have been provided in the field of mathematics by Dr Valerie Walkerdine and her colleagues (1981). More work is needed.

Let me return to curriculum metaphors. Here I am pleased to say that someone else has done much of the work. Robert Dearden has recently (1981) written a splendid paper about balance and coherence in the curriculum. Dearden has looked at the various official documents since 1977 about curriculum, and has examined some metaphorical uses: in particular, 'balance', 'coherence' and 'breadth'. One of his interesting points is that in this case the educational metaphors are resting upon metaphors already existing in other fields; so there is a double stretch involved. For example, if someone eats nothing but chips, then we might find useful in advising a change of habit, at a common-sense level, the metaphor of a 'balanced diet'. On closer inspection, however, the metaphor ceases to be so useful: balance implies some kind of equality, but no dietician suggests the merits of absorbing *equal* amounts of vitamins, proteins and minerals, etc. The compound metaphor of the *curriculum* as a balanced diet stretches credibility even further and is even more difficult to analyse. 'It is no more to be expected that the balanced curriculum will include equal amounts of science and swimming, or mathematics and poetry.' Dearden shows that this group of metaphors of 'balance', 'breadth' and 'coherence' depend on 'prior commitments'. Before we can agree upon what is a balanced curriculum, we must have a certain agreement about the components which are to be balanced and their relative value. We need 'some prior guidance on certain important points'. So, terms like coherence and balance raise more questions than they answer. They are secondary rather than primary principles, and it is no use appealing to the secondary principles until we have sorted out the primary.

Very often the use of the secondary principles such as 'balance' *assumes* that consensus exists at the primary principle level. But Dearden calls this into question, and I am sure he is right. These are not uncontroversial questions: they are not even clear issues. So when we talk of 'a balanced curriculum' or 'a coherent educational experience', we are begging very important questions and the metaphorical language is obscuring the real issue. The idea of a 'balanced diet' (in food) rests on certain reasonably well established scientific principles in nutrition about vitamins, proteins, etc. There is no such well established agreement about the various curricular ingredients.

The distressing feature of all the documents Dearden refers to is that they assume that this prior agreement exists, and therefore make no attempt to justify the compulsory inclusion of mathematics, science and a modern language, before going on to advocate the secondary idea of a satisfactory mixture, misleadingly referred to as 'balanced'. So we have here a group of metaphors with very limited powers of illumination, which at certain levels may well mislead.

Now for another category of curriculum metaphor, where there is not only a lack of illumination as in 'a balanced curriculum', but a serious and potentially dangerous error.

My particular *bête noire* (if you do not mind a French metaphor for a change) is the use of 'objectives' in curriculum planning. It is now very common on both sides of the Atlantic to assume that curriculum planning must involve objectives. In some ways this metaphor is similar to my earlier category of metaphors which start by being helpful, but at some point become misleading. The 'goal' or 'objective' metaphor has very little clarifying power, however. If a teacher has so little idea about what he should be doing in the classroom that he needs to think this out, then it might help to say 'what are your objectives?', although it might be equally helpful to say 'what are you trying to do?' The trouble with the objectives metaphor is that it is over-specific: an objective is a clear and *limited* educational intention indicating not only a direction but a finishing point, whereas the essence of education is that it is open ended. In other words, one of the problems with an objective is that it is not another way of saying 'be clear about what you are trying to teach'; it is much more specific than that — not least because some influential theorists (Popham, 1969; and Mager, 1962, for example) have deliberately defined objectives in terms of behavioural change. For them the only acceptable definition of an objective is that it must involve a pre-specified change in pupil behaviour which can be measured. In the early 1960s, there was a kind of educational puritanism in the United States — a movement dedicated to talk only in terms of behavioural objectives. Participants at curriculum conferences even sported car stickers and lapel badges saying 'Down with non-behavioural objectives!'

The philosophical objections to this point of view have been argued at length by Sockett (1980), Stenhouse (1975) and others. Their arguments justify my assertion that the objectives metaphor is not simply unhelpful, but dangerously wrong. If it is wrong, then why has it been incorporated into so much curriculum planning? Technician Education Council and Business Education Council curricular plans are based on the assumption that syllabus must be expressed in terms of objectives, and so are many Council for National Academic Awards and some Open University courses.

The problem is that at instructional levels of curriculum planning, to state precise objectives might be useful (Eisner, 1969, has written helpfully on this point). When teaching a skill such as typewriting it *might* make good sense to say that at the end of a six-week typing course a student should be able to type 'x' words a minute with only 'y' errors. (But only a fool would engage a secretary on typing skills alone.) There may even be important instructional levels within the educational process when objectives are useful — for example, the new graded tests in modern language learning seem sensible, and there are many other examples in elementary arithmetic or in laboratory safety skills. But as soon as you get beyond the basic skills to higher levels of educational processes and content, then limited objectives become not only misleading, but dangerous. Objectives can be useful in teaching spelling, but who would be bold enough to list what you or I should experience when reading Donne or seeing *Hamlet*? There is no one correct response or right interpretation.

One of the problems in curriculum planning is that a helpful procedure in one part of the curriculum or one level simply does not work in another subject, or at another level. And that applies to metaphors too. Because sequence is very important in mathematics, we should not assume that you must read Chaucer before Shakespeare; the spiral curriculum may be appropriate in some contexts, but not in others. The objectives metaphor implies that an educational experience is a goal to be reached; whereas for a fully educational experience the sky must be the limit. There is no end, no goal, no objective. It may be appropriate to have objectives on the way, but not as a finishing point.

Let me stay with the objectives example in relating some curriculum metaphors to ideologies on the one hand, and to practice on the other.

I have argued that the objectives myth has been widely accepted because of its usefulness at the instructional level, but that it is less useful (and perhaps no use at all) at higher levels of educational planning. But there is more to it than that. The objectives idea has strong ideological connections which make it very attractive to some educational and political decision makers (*not* necessarily consciously; I am not proposing some kind of conspiracy theory!). The ideological connections are important because they do tend to make a difference in practice as well as in theory.

I want first to put the objectives metaphor into a socio-historical context. The objectives view of curriculum planning may be traced back to Franklin Bobbitt, who began writing in 1918 on this subject, but it had been employed a little earlier specifically to apply the industrial ideas of F.W. Taylor (1856-1915) to the world of education. F.W. (Speedy) Taylor will be known to many of you as the industrial psychologist who improved the 'efficiency' of factories in America in the 1880s by 'scientific' management, that is, by close observation of workers, identifying and eliminating wasted time and motion. Part of the technique was to divide any job into a series of 'steps' each carefully timed with a stop watch. One of Speedy Taylor's contributions was that he brought a quantitative approach to the organization of production. Taylor's objective was to achieve more rational (another metaphorical term worthy of analysis) utilization of human and material resources at the workplace. He believed that for every task there was one — and only one — best way of doing it. Many writers have since pointed out that Taylor tended to treat human beings as extensions to the machinery, ignoring psychological and sociological features of work. Despite the inadequacies of Taylorism even as an aspect of mass production, it was thought desirable to apply it to education. Why? One answer is probably the desire for value for money at a time when, as now, costs were rising and resources were being limited; but that is in itself an aspect of an ideological position. After a lull in the Thirties and Forties the objectives school revived in the early 1950s. Tyler (1949) and Bloom (1956) were key figures. Mager and Popham were also in the forefront of this movement.

By the Fifties the background ideology included not only capitalist mass production, but also behaviourist psychology. Others such as Sockett (1980) have pointed out the philosophical error of this position and the essentially reductionist view of human behaviour which is associated with it. The objectives metaphor, despite its claims to be ideologically neutral is, in fact, an expression of behaviourist psychology and a mechanistic view of man. It is essentially a conservative doctrine because it is concerned with teaching the existing curriculum more efficiently, rather than calling it into question.

In practice it tends to be associated with testing and measuring the output rather than improving the quality of the input, and is arguably a very dangerous metaphor disguising an even more dangerous educational ideology.

Let me finally turn to a very different metaphor and a very different ideology, namely the idea of the curriculum as a process of cultural reproduction, and the so-called correspondence theory associated with this view. These are examples of what I referred to earlier as radical metaphors. I am personally more favourable disposed to radical change in education than to the conservative ideology I have just criticized. But it is just as necessary to look carefully at the way metaphors may distort arguments for change. Perhaps the most famous curriculum metaphor of all is constituted by the fable of the 'sabre-tooth' curriculum. It is so well known that I need only give a brief outline of it. The story goes that there was once a tribe in which the young were trained to spear fish for food and protect themselves by lighting fires to frighten away the sabre-toothed tiger. All went well for many years, until the climate changed and the streams became muddy so that the fish could no longer be speared; at the same time the sabre-toothed tiger disappeared and was replaced by a new enemy, the big brown bear which was not frightened of fires. So the technology changed. Nets were now invented to catch fish, and pits were dug to catch the brown bears. But, of course, schools carried on teaching about spearing fish and lighting fires. Eventually, a radical educationist appeared who suggested that schools should no longer teach these outdated skills, but should concentrate on net making and pit digging. But he was told that would not be education: that would be vocational training! And in any case, the curriculum was already overcrowded.

Relating that fable usually gets a laugh and makes the useful point that curricula all over the world tend to be somewhat out of date as a result of cultural lag and curriculum inertia (another two nice metaphors). But if we leave it at that, then the metaphor is misleading: is education to be no more than vocational training? Is there no value at all in traditional culture as opposed to modern technology?

The general tendency of such a radical metaphor is blanket and often an unargued condemnation of the old as of no value at all. Computer studies must simply replace classics and humanities; the metaphor tells us so, unequivocally.

There are, of course, many examples of this kind, sometimes accompanied by argument, but one that is often incomplete and which fails to invoke sufficient evidence. The metaphor is left with too much work to do. The metaphor of curriculum as cultural reproduction is one such example.

Bourdieu (1977) argues that schools are middle-class institutions designed to reproduce middle-class culture; working-class children tend to fail because they do not bring with them the 'cultural capital' possessed by middle-class children. I will not embark upon a criticism of this view. I simply want to point out some of the difficulties surrounding the two metaphors 'cultural reproduction' and 'cultural capital'.

'Cultural reproduction' gives the impression that the educational process is an all-or-nothing question: reproduction either takes place or it doesn't! Total success or total failure. This would seem to be both lacking in a sense of reality and extremely fatalistic: back to the predestination of the pure Calvinists — you are destined either to be saved or to be damned, and no amount of good work will save you. This is objectionable (apart from the question of the lack of evidence) for two reasons: first, it neglects or ignores the essential social interaction in the educational process, and it also ignores the fact that we are not either educated or uneducated; we are all somewhere on a continuum, and a continuum without a fixed point at the positive end.

The use of the subordinate metaphor 'cultural capital' is also significant. It suggests that some have something which they ought not to have, and it implies that once you have capital it will *automatically* pay a percentage in dividend or interest. It treats education as a commodity rather than a social process.

Another variation of this view is that of Bowles and Gintis (1976), in their use of correspondence theory. I will quote briefly from the now well-known book *Schooling in Capitalist America*, to give the flavour of a text, much of which I would agree with.

> The educational system helps integrate youth into the economic system, we believe, through a structural correspondence between its social relations and those of production. The structure of social relations in education not only inures the student to the discipline of the workplace, but develops the types of personal demeanour, modes of self-presentation, self-image, and social-class identifications which are the crucial ingredients of job adequacy. Specifically, the social relationships of education — the relationships between administrators and teachers, teachers and students, students and students, and students and their work — replicate the hierarchical division of labour. Hierarchical relations are reflected in the vertical authority lines from administrators to teachers to students. Alienated labour is reflected in the student's lack of control over his or her education, the alienation of the student from the curriculum content, and the motivation of school work through a system of grades and other external rewards rather than the student's integration with either the process (learning) or the outcome (knowledge) of the educational 'production process'. Fragmentation in work is reflected in the institutionalized and often

destructive competition among students through continual and ostensibly meritocratic ranking and evaluation. By attuning young people to a set of social relationships similar to those of the workplace, schooling attempts to gear the development of personal needs to its requirements. (Bowles and Gintis, 1976, p. 131)

My criticism of this view is limited to its use of metaphor. On a wider front, Edwards has, for example, complained of a lack of historical perspective in those English writers who have taken on board the American evidence and applied it to the English scene, also accusing Bowles and Gintis of 'flamboyant functionalism in which, like some piece of Gothic architecture, the strengths and weaknesses of the style are clearly in view' (Edwards, 1980, p. 67).

The problem of the radical metaphor is basically twofold: the metaphor of correspondence is given too much work to do and, therefore, clarity is lost; it is taken to mean not only that levels of schooling correspond to social-class levels, but also that the schooling which is provided corresponds to the needs of society, especially capitalist industry.

Bowles and Gintis in their 1980 reply to critics attempt to clarify their position, but still make the mistake of over-working the metaphor. One of the criticisms was that evidence was lacking which related the school to the needs of the workplace: that is, they failed to identify the *mechanisms* whereby economic interests are translated into educational programme. It was all very well stating this relationship as an assumption, but exactly how does the process work in practice? Bowles and Gintis argue that:

> the current relationship between education and economy is ensured not through the content of education but its form: the social relations of the educational encounter. Education prepares students to be workers through a correspondence between the social relations of production and the social relations of education. Like the division of labour in the capitalist enterprise, the educational system is a finely graded hierarchy of authority and control in which competition rather than co-operation governs the relations among participants, and an external reward system — wages in the case of the economy and grades in the case of schools — holds sway. This correspondence principle explains why the schools cannot at the same time promote full personal development and social equality, while integrating students into society. The hierarchical order of the school system, admirably geared towards preparing students for their future positions in the hierarchy of production, limits the development of those personal capacities involving the exercise of reciprocal and mutual democratic participation and reinforces social inequality by legitimating the assignment of students to inherently unequal 'slots' in the social hierarchy. (Bowles and Gintis, 1980, pp. 52 and 53)

This seems to claim that the content of the curriculum is not important; everything depends on the social relations. But the trouble is that social relations are much more difficult to identify and quantify. The metaphor makes the wages of work correspond to school grades, for example. But how? The metaphor is used as though it were proving a point when, in fact, evidence is almost totally lacking. Part of Edwards's cautionary discussion of Bowles and Gintis (and others who attempt to relate macro explanations of society to the micro analysis of classroom behaviour) is to commend to sociologists one of the working rules of historians: i.e., that there is no harm in attempting to apply a theory to an historical period so long as you do not close your eyes to contrary evidence or examples. He reminds us of Marc Bloch's assertion that sociologists had made room for history among the human sciences only to 'relegate it to one poor corner' of the room. Having reserved for themselves 'everything that appears susceptible to rational analysis', the sociologists shut up in the historical corner all those facts 'which they condemn as the most superficial and capricious' (Edwards, 1980, p. 73)

Some metaphors do have an influence on practice. The objectives metaphor which I criticized earlier has the effect of limiting objectives and converting education into a closed process rather than an open-ended experience. Curricula tend to become rigid and geared to measurement rather than development. Similarly, the radical metaphors of cultural reproduction and correspondence theory can have a depressing effect on teachers. There is nothing, according to Bowles and Gintis, that teachers can do to prevent education being the tool of a bourgeois society. However hard teachers may try, they will still end up by producing the kind of human beings that a capitalist society needs.

Last time I was in Strasbourg I had a couple of hours to spare and looked around the cathedral, which has an enormously tall spire. I bought a guide book and discovered that, during the Napoleonic wars, one particularly zealous officer in charge of the occupying revolutionary troops wanted to pull down the spire because it offended against the principle of equality. It was only with difficulty that the local townspeople persuaded him to express his egalitarian views in less permanent ways. The trouble is, in other words, that people take some metaphors and symbols seriously.

I am not, of course, claiming that all curriculum metaphors are as powerful as the radical and conservative ideological metaphors which I have identified. As I suggested earlier, some of them are simply misleading; others encourage us to make assumptions and beg questions when we ought to be seeking evidence or justification. I am not making a plea for the exclusion of metaphor in curriculum discussion. This would not only be impossible, as David Aspin has pointed out, but would also tend to impoverish our use of language if we tried. I am merely suggesting that we ought to be very careful in the way in which we use metaphors and equally cautious in accepting the metaphorical language of others — especially if we suspect that there may be an ideological wolf lurking in the metaphorical sheep's clothing.

Chapter Seven
Metaphors in Science and Education
Gerald Holton

All reflection, thought and criticism began in comparison, analogy and metaphor. Faust was wrong: in the beginning was not the act. St. John was right: in the beginning was the word. We are concerned with man, and the world can only exist for man as man knows or imagines it. Metaphor is the route of reason, science and art. (Donald G. MacRae, 1975, p. 59.)

Analogy: . . . a form of reasoning that is particularly liable to yield false conclusions from true premisses. (Alan Bullock and Oliver Stallybrass, 1977, p. 20.)

In your invitation to address myself to metaphors in science and education, I detected a hope that I might sidestep the battles about the theories of metaphor from Aristotle to our day, and also not go again over the ground of fine distinctions between metaphor, model, analogy, simile, and all the other tools for performing imitative magic. Rather, my contribution would centre on praxis. In drafting this chapter on metaphors in science and education, I soon saw I would have to take off from illustrative examples of the roles metaphor can have for good or ill, first of all in the actual work of scientists. When we know whether and how metaphor lives within the laboratory, and diffuses from there into the wider world, we might begin to discern what the educator must do about it. Even if one adds the limitation that of necessity I limit myself chiefly to physical sciences and slight the others, I still find myself with a vast topic for which I can sketch out here only some of the interesting problems.

To the first question then: Does modern science, properly conducted, really have anything profound to do with metaphor? It will not be universally granted that it has. Ever since Francis Bacon, the use of metaphor has tended to be an embarrassment to some scientists and philosophers. Bacon allowed that metaphors might be 'anticipations of nature', but on the whole he dismissed them as serving the 'idols' and our natural penchant for fantasy.

Today, those who consider themselves to be the last defenders of the age of reason and inheritors of the battle flags of the old positivism would rather stress scientific discourse in the form of protocol sentences. On this view, good scientific concepts are operational, fairly unambiguously shared by the worldwide community of scientists. Their meaning is as clear as human language can get. Scientists, they will say, differ from humanistic scholars by keeping fundamental decisions free from essentially psychological (aesthetic or intuitive) or external (sociological) influences, and let themselves be guided only by the empirical data and logical machinery. On the other hand, metaphors by definition are flexible, subject to a variety of personal interpretations, and often the results of an overburdened imagery. At best, they might be used informally in the classroom or, with caution, in the textbooks. They are part of the natural armamentarium of the artist, poet, or critic, but not of the working scientist.

And it is not only those watchdogs of proper rationality in science who express alarm. Even Colin Turbayne, in his useful *The Myth of Metaphor*, reserved his first and longest case to an exposure of the great harm he considers to have been done to Western thought by the false use of metaphors in the thinking of great scientists. Mechanism is, he said,

> a case of being victimized by metaphor. I choose Descartes and Newton as excellent examples of metaphysicians of mechanism *malgré eux*, that is to say, as unconscious victims of the metaphor of the great machine. Together they have founded a church, more powerful than that founded by Peter and Paul, whose dogmas are now so entrenched that anyone who tries to reallocate the facts is guilty of more than heresy . . . (Turbayne, 1962, p. 5)

But the implied dichotomy between good metaphor and good science, while widespread, is a vast oversimplification. Comparative linguists have amply demonstrated that our store of metaphors and other imaginative devices determines to a large extent what we can think in any field. Further evidence comes from the findings of historians of science. Their work has shown that fundamentally thematic decisions, even though usually made unconsciously, frequently map out the shape of theories within which scientists progress.

Indeed, it is not too much to say that modern science began with a quarrel over a metaphor. Nicolaus Copernicus, in the first sentence of the introduction to Book I of *De Revolutionibus*, stated his belief that 'The strongest affection and utmost zeal' is reserved for the promotion of 'the studies concerned with the most beautiful objects.' Those are the proper subjects of astronomy, 'the discipline which deals with the universe's God-like circular movements, and which explains its whole appearance. What indeed is more beautiful than heaven, which of course contains all things of beauty?' This vision provided him, Copernicus says, 'extraordinary intellectual pleasure', even as 'the Godly psalmist . . . rejoiced in the works of His hands'.

But in this realm of divine Beauty, there had appeared a Beast, and Copernicus saw it as his high task to chase it out. As he explains in the preface:

> Those who devised the eccentrics [for modelling the motion of planets] seem thereby in large measure to have solved the problem of the apparent motions with appropriate calculations. But meanwhile they introduced a good many ideas [— such as the equant] which apparently contradict the first principles of uniform motion. Nor could they elicit or deduce from the eccentrics the principal consideration, that is, the structure of the universe and the true symmetry of its parts. On the contrary, their experience was just like someone taking from various places hands, feet, a head, and other pieces, very well depicted it may be, but not for the representation of a single person; since these fragments would not belong to one another at all, *a monster rather than a man* would be put together from them. (Copernicus, 1978 trans., pp. 4–7; my italic)

There is some disagreement among historians about the precise nature of the monster, but the main point is clear: The hand of God is not the hand of Dr. Frankenstein who, in Mary Shelley's romance, assembles his monster also out of incongruous parts. To reassert the reign of beauty, Copernicus goes back to what he had called 'the first principles of uniform motion'. He rejects non-uniformities and inconstancies of motion — his 'mind shudders' at the very consideration of them — and even at the cost of setting the earth into motion, he arrives at a system that has all the earmarks of divine handicraft: the equants are gone, the phenomena are saved; the whole system has symmetry, parsimony, necessity. Indeed, contemplating it as if he himself were viewing it from above, Copernicus is moved to exclaim, at the end of chapter 10, in a moment of uncontrolled enthusiasm: 'So vast, without any question, is the divine handiwork of the most excellent Almighty.' It was one of the few sentences which the censor of the Inquisition in 1616 insisted on striking out.

But it was too late. The device of uniform motion in a circle was not forced by the data; and as Kepler's ellipsi showed later, it was not even the most functional device from the mathematical point of view. Yet the metaphor of uniform circular motion as the divine key for solving the problems posed by the phenomena — even as in antiquity — had infected the thinking from which the scientific revolution of the seventeenth century came. At the very least, the case shows that the function of a metaphor need not be merely, as in Aristotle, a transfer of meaning, but can be 'a restructuring of the world', in the words of Sir Ernst Gombrich (1972, p. 166).

In trying to account for Galileo's irrational refusal to accept Keplerian ellipsi (and with them, the additional proofs of the heliocentric system which Galileo was so passionately defending), Alexandre Koyré coined the memorable phrase *hantise de la circularité*; and Erwin Panofsky (1956) made the case that this spell of circularity on Galileo was equally at work in his physics and in his aesthetic judgements in the arts. In what follows we shall have to come back to at least a few points that have here only been touched on lightly. But the vanquishing of the monster and the triumph of the divine circle remind us that metaphors do not have to be casual indulgences: they can help to make, and defend, a world view.

Lest it be thought that such examples characterized science only in its early stages, let me draw attention to more recent ones. In Thomas Young's 1804 'Reply to the Animadversions of the Edinburgh Reviewers', he announced the idea for which he is best known, namely that light is fundamentally a wave phenomenon. As he put it, 'light is a propagation of an impulse communicated to [the] ether by luminous bodies' (Young, 1804, p. 80). He reminds his reader that 'It has already been conjectured by Euler, that [contrary to Newton] the colours of light consist in the different frequency of the vibrations of the luminous ether.' (ibid., p. 81) But this had been only a speculation: Young says 'It does not appear that he has supported this opinion by any argument.' And now follows, in a half sentence, the first statement of Thomas Young's striking proposal:

> but it [the idea 'that light is a propagation of an impulse to the ether'] is strongly confirmed, by the analogy between the colours of a thin plate and the sounds of a series of organ pipes (ibid.).

Even before we look at the details of this analogy, we feel the almost breathtaking daring of this transference of meaning between what were previously two entirely separate phenomena. Indeed, the courage for such a jump seemed so ill-advised to George Peacock, devoted friend and editor of Thomas Young's *Works*, when he assembled the volume in 1855, twenty-six years after the death of Young and long after the firm establishment of the wave theory, that he felt he must save the reader from some dreadful mistake; and so George Peacock, D.D., 'Dean of Ely, Lowndean Professor of Astronomy in the University of Cambridge, and formerly Fellow and

Tutor of Trinity College, FRS, FGS, FRAS,' etc., etc., adds, as a stern footnote that is perhaps unique in the literature: 'This analogy is fanciful and altogether unfounded. Note by the Editor.'

The good Dean, having been taught in the meanwhile by Arago and Fresnel that light waves are transverse rather than longitudinal, perhaps saw more clearly the differences than the similarities. But if we return to the historical situation, as we can with the aid of the details given by Thomas Young, we are struck by the genius that allowed him to make the jump. During his early years at Cambridge, Young had done experiments toward an understanding of the human voice, and for that purpose had studied the way sound is produced in organ pipes. Strangely enough, the subject was in a rather confused state, and it was in fact Thomas Young who proposed the law of superposition which allows one to understand the action of organ pipes in terms of the interference between sound waves travelling in opposite directions within the pipe. He had noted that 'The same sound — for example middle C — could be obtained by means of a uniform blast, from organ pipes which are different multiples of the same length.' If you stood in front of a series of such pipes, whose lengths are as 1 to 2 to 3 to 4, etc., and if some skilful person blows the different pipes in turn and produces the same note, you would know that the mechanism by which organ pipes work, no matter what the details may be, is very likely to be a wave phenomenon; for it will conjure up in your mind the traditional distributions of nodes and anti-nodes on the model of interfering waves, whether they be longitudinal or transverse.

Now, to go to the other part of the offensive half-sentence, that is, from 'the sounds of a series of organ pipes' to 'the colours of a thin plate'. Thomas Young had found in Newton's *Opticks* the beautiful description of the experiments on thin plates and Newton's rings. You will recall that if two thin plates of glass are set up at a slight angle from each other, so that there is a gradually increasing wedge of air between them, and if light of a given colour is allowed to fall on the arrangement, the eye placed above the plates observes equally spaced bands of colour return to it from the wedge. The height of the air wedge formed by the two glass plates, at the point from which light is returned, is as 1 to 2 to 3 to 4, etc. As Thomas Young puts it, 'The same color recurs whenever the thickness answers to the terms of an arithmetical progression.' And he immediately tells us the point on which the metaphor depends: 'Now this is precisely similar to the production of the same sound, by means of a uniform blast, from organ pipes which are different multiples of the same length.'

We can almost see him standing over the thin plates in the optical experiment, looking at the light displayed at equal distances in the same colour, and exclaiming — as one would have to do now if one had not thought of it before — that regardless of detailed mechanism, this must be a wave phenomenon.

Of course he has all the details wrong. Not only is light transverse, which would make little difference to his argument, but the colours seen in the thin plates, even though an interference phenomenon, are not due to a standing wave, as for sound in the organ pipes. Also, there are no pipes in the case of light. But all this is quite secondary and irrelevant. The main thing was his ability to perceive 'the analogy between the colours of a thin plate and the sounds of a series of organ pipes'. Contrary to George Peacock, you know that if a student, previously ignorant of all these matters, comes to you with the discovery of such analogy, you would be delighted and put him at once to work on your lab. team.

I regard the case of Thomas Young as an exemplar of the creative function of metaphor in the nascent phase of the scientific imagination. Anyone who has known or studied scientists at the highest level of achievement knows of this mechanism. Faraday's notebooks are full of it, as is Maxwell's work. For Fermi it was part of his scientific credo to use and re-use the same ideas in quite different settings; for example, a year and a half after a paper dealing with the effect of slow electrons, Fermi was in the unique position of thinking about the effect of slow *neutrons* when his team, evidently by accident, came upon the artificial radioactivity of silver (produced by scattered neutrons).

But of all such examples my favourite is still an autobiographical passage I found some years ago, in Einstein's own hand, in the copy of an unpublished manuscript dating from about 1919 or shortly afterwards, located at the Einstein Archives in Princeton. The title of the document (in translation) is 'Fundamental Ideas and Methods of Relativity Theory, Presented in their Development'. There, in the middle of a technical paper, Einstein writes suddenly, in a personal way about what he called 'the happiest thought of my life'[1] which came to him in 1907 and opened the way to go from special to general relativity. He explained in 1919:

> As with the electric field produced by electro-magnetic induction [1905], the gravitational field has similarly only a relative existence. For if one considers an observer in free fall, e.g., from the roof of a house, there exists for him during his fall no gravitational field — at least in his immediate vicinity. (Quoted in Holton, 1979, pp. 363–4)

If we analyze this passage (which is quite coherent with other reports

Einstein gave of his thoughts in the matter), we see a number of parallels with the case of Thomas Young. Now the gulf to be negotiated by a metaphoric transference is between the electric and magnetic fields on the one hand, and the gravitation field on the other. The 'happiest thought' in 1907, which led indeed to a restructuring of our world picture, was really a simple extension of the analogy from uniform motion in a magnetic field to accelerated motion in a gravitational field — although from the point of view of the physics of the time the analogy might indeed also have been called 'fanciful and altogether unfounded'.

An earlier passage in the same Einstein manuscript brings us to a point that also has to be discussed, namely, the possible motivation for risking the metaphor. Such risks (which Einstein took repeatedly in his scientific papers) are not made playfully or by accident. The urges to find analogies, and thereby to simplify and unify the various branches of a science, are actively at work in the background of the research of these explorers. In a famous note written to himself on March 19, 1849, Faraday enters the experimental search for a link between gravity and electric and magnetic phenomena with the sentence, twice underlined, 'All this is a dream.' The dream comes first. Or a nightmare: Einstein, recalling once more the distaste with which he beheld the physics before 1905, in which the current in a conductor induced by a magnet in motion relative to it was thought to be the result of quite different physical effects, depending on whether the magnet or the conductor was regarded as 'really' at rest, exclaims in his 1919 manuscript:

> The thought that one is dealing here with two fundamentally different cases was for me unbearable [*war mir unerträglich*]. The difference between these two cases could not be a real difference, but only a difference in the choice of the reference point.

In this mood, the metaphor is a godsent means for bridging an apparent but 'unbearable' gulf.

In stressing this active and creative side of metaphoric thinking, I do not want to be misunderstood as giving a normative analysis of recommended scientific procedure. I would rather look at the record to see what did happen. Also, I know well that the cases of brilliant success do not imply that there have been no failures — either a new metaphor misused, or an old, seemingly 'dead' but still powerful, metaphor falsely accepted. A case of that latter sort is surely the inability of a group of experimentalists in the 1920s to come upon parity violation in their own data on the asymmetry of the scattering of electrons. The parity and isotropy observed throughout physics at that time forced itself also upon their imagination in this case, and helped them and all others who looked at the data at the time to find an easier way out.

I shall treat later cases of surprising metaphor excess and its costs. But the essentially constructive role metaphor has usually played in the making of science is clear. In a recent article, Andy Pickering of Edinburgh writes: 'Wherever one looks in the history of particle physics, one sees this magical transmutation, producing new theories from old through a process of analogical recycling.' He concludes:

> I have been trying to suggest that it would be useful to replace the idea that scientists are the passive *discoverers* of the unproblematic facts of nature with the alternative view that they actively *construct* their world. (Pickering, 1980)

We see here too a disagreement with the opposing traditions that stress the passive role of metaphor, as expressed for example by Richard Boyd (in the volume *Metaphor and Thought*, edited by Ortony):

> Neither do we, in any important sense, 'construct' the world when we adopt linguistic or theoretical frameworks. Instead *we* accommodate *our* language to the structure of a theory-independent world. (Boyd, 1979, p. 408)

I have asserted that in the work of the active scientist there are not merely *occasions* for using metaphor, but *necessities* for doing so, as when trying to remove an unbearable gap or monstrous fault. I now turn at least briefly to these necessities, and first of all the necessity built into the process of scientific rationality itself, an epistemological necessity that favours the search for and use of metaphors. It is simply the limitation of induction. Where logic fails, analogic continues. The bridge is now made no longer of steel but of gossamer. It breaks often, but sometimes it carries us across the gulf; and in any case there is nothing else that will. In several papers, I have recently been exploring the existence of discontinuities that appear in scientific theory construction, forcing what Einstein[2] repeatedly called the researcher's 'widely speculative' or 'groping constructive attempt', or even a desperate proposal made when one has given up finding other paths to an overarching axiom system. A second discontinuity, Einstein noted, lies in the fact that we often select concepts without some logical necessity, really 'arbitrarily'; 'considered logically, the concept is not identical with the totality of sense impression referred to; but it is a free creation of the human (or animal) mind.' Indeed, the whole 'system of concepts is a creation of man', achieved in a 'free play'.

For these reasons, Einstein warned strongly against making the mistake to think of concepts as being the result of 'abstraction' from observation. Eventually, Einstein developed a theory of levels, or 'stratification of the scientific system' in which the discontinuities between strata draw attention to the need for some sort of creative groping across the discontinuity that is often helped by resort to metaphor. He held that in the striving for logical unity, the theorist is progressively led from a 'first layer' to a 'secondary system' and on to higher levels, each characterized by more parsimony in concepts and relations, and particularly in the concepts directly connected with complexes of sense experience. 'So one continues until we have arrived at a system of the greatest conceivable unity, and of the greatest conceptual paucity of the logical foundations that is compatible with the nature of what is given to our senses' — even though there is no guarantee that 'this greatest of all aims can really be attained to a very high degree'.

A further necessity for the resort to metaphor in the nascent phase of science-making is precisely what troubled Francis Bacon: the habits and irresistible play of our imagination, and often the imagination in its blatantly anthropomorphic form. While there are good social covenants for removing all traces in the pedagogical recasting of scientific achievement after the imaginative act is over, the making of science presupposes life-world experience. As Immanuel Kant noted, the imagination does not distinguish between life-world experience [*lebensweltliche Erfahrung*] and scientific experience. This is now not a judgement, but an ethno-methodological fact, derived from observing scientists at work. They can't help themselves. Thus, Millikan was so convinced of the existence of the discrete corpuscle of unitary electric charge that he wrote about it, in his autobiography as if he had seen it with his own eyes: 'He who has seen that experiment, and hundreds of investigators have observed it, [has] in effect SEEN the electron.' When the droplet he was observing in the electric field was changing speed, an image came quickly to mind, and he wrote: 'One single electron jumped upon the drop. Indeed, we could actually see the exact instant at which it jumped on or off.' Rutherford told Millikan: 'Ions are jolly little beggars, you can almost see them.' And at about the time Millikan began to 'see' his electrons, Jean Perrin, battling for the acceptance of atomicity of matter, held that a refusal to believe in the atom because of its invisibility was 'puerile anthropomorphism'. Mary Jo Nye has observed that one student wrote of Perrin: 'He "sees" atoms — there is no doubt at all — as Saint Thomas saw seraphim.' (Holton, 1978, pp. 37–8)

In the privacy of the laboratory, and sometimes, less cautiously, even in publication, the 'idols', and particularly the idol of the theatre, play their necessary role, with all the dangers and benefits that this may imply. In a frank and personal essay, Martin Deutsch (1958), the nuclear physicist at M.I.T., has discussed 'the striking degree to which an experimenter's preconceived image of the process which he is investigating determines the outcome of his observations', and particularly the 'symbolic anthropomorphic representation of the basically inconceivable atomic processes':

> The human imagination, including the creative scientific imagination, can ultimately function only by evoking potential or imagined sense impressions . . . I confess I have never met an experimental physicist who does not think of the hydrogen atom by evoking a visual image of what he would see if the particular atomic model with which he is working existed literally on a scale accessible to sense impressions — even while realizing that in fact the so-called internal structure of the hydrogen atom is *in principle* inaccessible to direct sensory perception. This situation has far-reaching consequences for the method of experimental investigation. (Deutsch, 1958, pp. 88–9)

A number of things have come together here — angels to keep company with our earlier monster, the anthropomorphic kernel in a science which, as Einstein often said, was itself a way of getting beyond 'the merely personal', and the role of visualization. I come back to the role of visualization in what follows, but must stop to comment at this point. On this, again, I turn to Gombrich (1972). He notes that the linear character of language makes it hard to hold in mind some concepts that become quite evident when put in diagrammatic form. 'This may be one of the psychological reasons for our instinctive equation between seeing and understanding.' And he quotes a passage from Cicero on the special appeal of the immediacy of sight:

> Every metaphor, provided it is a good one, has a direct appeal to the senses, especially the sense of sight, which is the keenest: for while the rest of the senses apply such metaphors as . . . 'the softness of a humane spirit', 'the roar of the sea' and 'the sweetness of speech', the metaphors drawn from the sense of sight are much more vivid, almost placing before the mind's eye what we cannot discern and see. (Gombrich, 1972, p. 167)

If we had a categorization of scientific metaphors, analogous to Stith Thompson's classification of themes in myth and folklore, or something like the *Atlas Mnemosyne* of Warburg, we would find that the longest sections would go to visualizable metaphors and to anthropomorphic and folkloric metaphors. Human life, the life cycle, and human relationships pervade, in sometimes only slightly disguised form, the most sophisticated scientific papers and, more so, our textbooks, 'Strange' particles decay and, in the spark chamber photograph or similar view field, are shown to give rise to new generations of particles, each with its own characteristic lifetime. We speak of families of radioactive isotopes, consisting of a parent, daughters, grand-daughters, etc. We constantly tell stories of evolution and devolution, of birth, adventure and death on the atomic, molar, or cosmic scale. The chemist's molecules are metamorphosed to enter the life-history of another chemical species. I have always felt it ironic that particularly the newer sciences such as psychology and sociology tend to borrow their metaphors and other terminology so heavily from the older and more respectable physical sciences when, in fact, those have been deriving them in the first place from the most primitive and familiar experiences.

The metaphors based on the human body are undoubtedly the most numerous and seductive in the sciences because, as Vico put it, man is 'buried in the body'. Donald MacRae is surely right when he says,

> If we are to understand the body as metaphor, and as source of metaphors derivable directly or by transformation rules from it, we must remember that our own experience of our bodies is prescientific. (MacRae, 1975, p. 67)

This applies both to the metaphors which work for us, and to those that eventually do not. Although he did not intend it, MacRae made this point too, and in a manner that brings our attention with uncanny accuracy back to something I discussed at the beginning: 'We make our monsters out of bodily parts.'

The fourth and last of the reasons why scientists find themselves forced to risk metaphoric thought has to do simply with the fast metabolism of science, so much faster now than for many other fields of thought and action. Scientific vocabulary and imagery are never stabilized. Scientists seem to be working at the edge of an ever more active volcano that showers them with novelties demanding neologisms at an ever increasing rate. At the same time, of course, old metaphors decay and are lost, or at least are apt to be misinterpreted. Thus the proton has betrayed its etymology by turning out not to be the first of things — and now it is even flirting with the idea of giving up its immortality, settling for a half-life of a mere 10^{32} years which will cause diamonds not to be forever. While Homer's Briseis of the fair cheek will remain tender forever in some circumlocution or other, the metaphors of science seem to have a shorter and shorter half-life of their own. And the conditions under which new ones are fashioned seem to verge now occasionally on the frenzy and informality of a big beer-drinking party. We are now invited to settle for quarks that combine the properties of flavour, charm, and 'bareness' with either 'truth' or 'beauty', or, in cruder terminology, with either 'top' or 'bottom'. Some of the metaphors are hammered together out of odd bits and pieces, without attention to delicacies of taste.

It struck me some time ago that since the turn of the century the terminology entering physical science often had a thematic root contrary to the older (and persisting) themata of hierarchy, continuity, and order. That is, the newer conceptions, perhaps corresponding to the characteristic style of our turbulent age, tend to be characterized by the antithetical thema of disintegration, violence, derangement. Evident examples are: radioactive decay, Principles of Impotency, displacement law, fission, spallation, nuclear disintegration, discontinuity (in energy levels), dislocation, indeterminacy, uncertainty, probabilistic causality, strangeness, quantum number, negative states, forbidden transitions, particle annihilation. It is indeed the terminology of a restless, even violent, world.

This brings us inevitably to consider, at least in a first pass, the student new to our classroom. One can say that all the necessities forcing scientists to use metaphors in their work become handicaps for students, who inherit all the troubles and none of the rewards.

Think of what is in the head of your new student, the 'metaphor background' and 'metaphor readiness'. Indeed, in the student's head there may be a disorderly mixture of new and old metaphoric terms. The Big Dipper, the black hole, the big bang, and the big crunch. The harmony of the spheres, the expanding universe, the clockwork universe, attraction and repulsion, inertia, perhaps Schrödinger's cat, left-handed neutrinos, parity breakdown, coloured and flavoured quarks, gluons, charm, and God playing (or not playing) dice. Also, the heat death, kingdoms of animals and plants, computers that crash or refuse commands, broken symmetry, families of elements, daughter and grand-daughter isotopes in radioactive decay, negative feedback, circulation of blood, the tangled bank, the selfish gene, degenerate quantum states, and 'everything is relative'. (If students go to Wheaton College in Boston, they may encounter a new course in biology being fashioned on radical feminist lines in which, for example, fertilization will be described as an encounter between an aggressive spermatozoon — an old stereotype — and an 'equally aggressive egg' that envelopes it, rather than passively accepting what comes.)

The main trouble with this *bouillabaisse* is that metaphors do not carry with them clear demarcations of the areas of their legitimacy. They may be effective tools for scientists, but pathetic fallacies for students. For the latter, the problem stems in good part from the sociology of communication. Margaret Mead (1959) noted more than twenty years ago that scientists at the frontier, where the terminology and imagery are developed, speak mostly to other scientists at or near their own level of understanding. In this way, scientific language has escaped from the realm of 'natural language'. This is the fate of 'any language taught only by adults to adults — or to children as if they were adults . . . It serves in the end primarily to separate those who know it from those who do not.' Since then, linguists and anthropologists have been reinforcing the point that the cure cannot come from simple 'translation' but may lie in recognizing that a difference in languages reflects a difference in world views. Without making the mutual accommodation of these views a prominent part of the agenda, science teaching probably has to remain superficial. I refer here to the work of R. Horton on African traditional thought and Western science, and of J. Jones in Margaret Mead's own New Guinea; both Horton and Jones have studied the ways in which the traditional cultures of the new learners differ from the scientific cultures of the teachers, and how and to what limited degree these differences can be decreased (see Logan, 1981).

The most serious charge one might make is that the negligence of scientists, in their role of teachers, to deal with this cultural difference may not be merely a shirking from an admittedly very difficult task. It may even be *functional*, as I shall note later.

Further examples of the powers and pitfalls of metaphors in science and education, are offered by relativity theory, and specifically the way the early researchers conceived of length contraction and time dilation. In H.A. Lorentz's and H. Poincaré's work, these were, of course, not symmetrical, but 'real' actions of the ether, that legacy of Greek, Cartesian and Newtonian physics. With Einstein, ether was dismissed as merely 'a substratum of nineteenth-century thought' (in the happy phrase of René Dugas). Possibly with the courage gathered by reading Ernst Mach's attack on absolute time and absolute space, Einstein relegated the ether into the dustbin of non-operational and therefore harmful conceptions (at least in the first decade of his work), and instead drew attention to the reality of the transformation equations themselves, including their implication of complete symmetry. But new metaphors rush in to take the place of old. Thus Minkowski announced in 1908 that 'from this hour on', space by itself and time by itself would become mere shadows, and only a sort of union of the two will maintain existence. What he called with great flamboyance 'the World' was now a kind of unchanging, crystalline structure in which all past and future processes are represented by lines and their intersections.

At about the same time, more metaphors grew around relativity theory, e.g., at the hand of Langevin, who introduced the 'twin paradox' in more or less its popular form. Thereby what had slumbered in neutral-looking transformation equations became the widely interesting matter of relative ageing, counting of heartbeats, and the like. Some of the literature of the times, both in scientific meetings (e.g., those of the Swiss Physics Society) and in the popular press, show how suddenly and vigorously interest was aroused by this extension of the metaphor to human life.

Another version of the same 'metaphor excess' had to do with the discussion given by Einstein in his popular book, and much used elsewhere, of length contraction, for example of the famous and easily visualizable train dashing through that railway station. The 'contraction' which previously had been thought to be real within the world view of ether physics was now thought. to be directly visible from any other co-ordinate system. Textbooks, popular articles, and even films began to represent the contraction. Both laymen and scientists seemed to see the contraction in simple and similar ways whenever they wanted to. For about forty-five years after Einstein's first publication, a cubical object, for example, moving at high speed across your line of sight was thought of as presenting itself as a rectangle, its shorter side in the direction of motion 'shrunk' by virtue of the length's contraction. But then, through the work of Terrell, Penrose and others in 1958–59, it became clear, to everyone's surprise, that an observer of a relativistic moving object would see not a distortion; rather, the object would appear not distorted but only rotated. The rotation, or rather 'remapping' upon the observer's screen, is itself a metaphor with rather unexplored limits.

A second example of an important metaphor in physical science is the circular, mandala-like construct (already mentioned in the early part of this paper in passing) as the solution for a great variety of problems. It often seems one might say in the physical sciences: 'The circle, or some modification of it, is the answer. What is your question?' This would take us from a common starting point into various directions. One is the Platonic-Aristotelian-Ptolemaic-Copernican-Tychonic . . . sequence. Then would follow the often painful modifications of the circle as a fundamental explanatory metaphor: Kepler's struggle with the ellipse; or Galileo's dismay on discovering that Saturn, far from being a round object, has ear-like appendages (that later were understood to be Saturn's rings, seen at a slowly changing angle through a poor telescope).

As it turned out, motion in a ring around Saturn was not unique in the solar system. Planetary rings were found to be quite commonplace, varying from substantial ones as for the main rings of Saturn or the rings of Uranus, to the more ephemeral dusty ring of Jupiter. Even now, a large and expensive project is trying to find rings around Neptune, on the assumption that the failures to find them so far are simply not credible. A self-respecting planet is now *supposed* to have rings.

The observation of two-dimensional rings around three-dimensional objects reminds us how strangely little resistance was offered to two-dimensional projections and indeed to two-dimensional models, for the purpose both of representation and of theoretical modelling, even in the discussion of the origins of the solar system. The constraints of the two-dimensional surface on which to draw or print must, after all, affect our thinking constantly. Depictions of Laplace's nebula hypothesis, or of T.C. Chamberlin's theory of planet production by the accretion of planetesimals in circular orbits, or of the patterns of motion in the solar nebula according to Weizsäcker's theory, etc., show how much at home we are with two-dimensional thinking for three-dimensional problems.

The penchant for two-dimensional thinking appears even stronger when we turn from the macroscopic mandala of the solar system to its microcosmic equivalent. Ringed Saturn shrank to atomic size when Nagaoka proposed it as a model of the atom in 1903, after having read Maxwell's paper on the stability of motion in Saturn's rings. Rutherford referred to it favourably in a letter and publication of 1911, about the time when he was being joined at his laboratory by Niels Bohr. The model contained a strongly charged central object, with a number of negative electrons of equal mass, arranged in a circle at equal angular intervals.

A rival model of the atom, also influential on physicists from 1911 on, was also frankly two-dimensional and indeed made its way into the physics literature through a lecture demonstration of magnet needles floating in a bowl of water placed below a large cylindrical magnet. Depending on their number, the magnet needles arrange themselves sooner or later in regular two-dimensional patterns. Now a rather familiar demonstration, it was new when published by the American physicist Alfred M. Mayer in *Silliman's American Journal* (Mayer, 1878), and the arrangement of the magnets, projected on a screen, made a big impression on students and popular audiences. They caught the attention of J.J. Thomson. Even the original manuscript pages of (largely two-dimensional) calculations and subsequent publications from Bohr through Sommerfeld, show the power of the Saturnian model, suitably but not essentially metamorphosed.

In retrospect it is rather astonishing how well these models worked, from explaining the Zeemann effect and some chemistry to the fine structure of spectral lines — astonishing, because of course it was, from the present point of view, completely wrong at the very point where the metaphor then used was most convincing: the axially symmetrical, easily visualizable playground of equally visualizable events. Between 1913 and 1927, the old, almost axiomatic *Anschaulichkeit* at the base of models, analogies, and other metaphors in the physical sciences had to be given up.

Though you cannot tell it from the representations in our introductory physics books of today, what Heisenberg achieved over a half a century ago was 'complete freedom from planetary orbits'. The principal problem with the sensual Kantian notion of *Anschaulichkeit* in the old quantum theory was that the *Anschauungen* were memories or abstractions from the world of perceptions, and consequently were encumbered with pictures that made sense only in terms of classical causality and conservation laws. It implied that matter is infinitely divisible in principle, and hence did not do justice in its very essence to the atomic regime with its discontinuities.

Other solutions to the puzzle of the atom were of course possible in principle. Thus A.N. Whitehead (1948, p. 105) suggested that the atom and molecule are to be considered analogous to biological entities, organisms rather than classical particles. And it is also worth noting that chemistry made do with linear or planar models until the 1870s. Structural theory in chemistry did not seriously use three-dimensional space until the 'tetra-hedronal carbon atom' was introduced by van't Hoff and le Bell.

The last of the three cases that deserves detailed analysis concerns the metaphoric descriptions of the *task* of the sciences and of what it is supposed to achieve when all is said and done. Immediately our imagination resonates to such images and metaphors as 'revolutions', voyages into the unknown, the voyeurist drawing aside of the veil covering Mother Nature, the great-mystery story view, the jigsaw puzzle view, the endless-horizon pursuit, and many others.

But the imagery which seems to be the most powerful and motivating one is that of the mountaineer gradually ascending, and thereby gaining not merely the conquest of the peak, but the aesthetic, largely visual thrill of an *overview*, encompassing the whole circular area below, from horizon to horizon, and, in the unearthly stillness at that high altitude, seeing at a glance the way the details of the landscape below fit together in one meaningful picture. It matches Bradley's famous definition of metaphysics as 'the effort to comprehend the universe not simply piecemeal or by fragments, but somehow as a whole'.

You will perceive that this image connects in various ways with matters I have discussed before: the planar and quasi-circular area of action, the importance of visualization, Einstein's 'layer theory' of higher, and more and more encompassing levels of theory perfection, with the attendant lengthening of the distance between the concepts and the 'facts' of the plane on which there is crowded the 'multiplicity of immediate sense experiences' — that plane, above which the system of axioms may be found in painful search. Einstein used that metaphor several times, with all the visual imagery typical of his writings. As he put it in his 1918 *Motiv des Forschens*, the pursuit of science is motivated first negatively, by the

> flight from the everyday life with its painful harshness and wretchedness, and from the fetters of one's own shifting desires . . . the longing that irresibly pulls a town-dweller toward the silent, high mountains, where the eye ranges freely through the still, pure air and traces the calm contours that seem to be made for eternity. (Holton, 1973, pp. 376-7)

A second, positive part of the motivation is that 'man seeks to form for himself, in whatever manner is suitable for him, a simplified and comprehensive picture of the world'. The achievement of such a *Weltbild* is in fact 'the supreme task of the physicist'. 'The longing to behold that pre-established harmony between the world of experience and the theoretical system is the source of the inexhausible perseverance and patience' of the researcher (ibid.).

We can trace the majestic metaphor of the *Weltbild* from Goethe, Schleiermacher and Alexander von Humboldt. Cassirer (1925) put it succinctly: a characteristic and typical *Weltbild* is formed when the chaos of sense impression is arranged into a cosmos. During the first two decades of the twentieth century, the fight over the 'unity' of the physical *Weltbild* was intense among German scientists. We have become more modest (or more pedestrian) in our descriptive language, even though our colleagues are getting Nobel prizes for their inexorable climb towards the Grand Unification Theories of all the forces of Nature. Current discussions about the ultimate attainment of a unified and coherent world picture in the physical sciences do allow us to discern echoes and overtones from those earlier debates when the context of a near-sacred mission was never entirely hidden. Scientists used to lapse into poetry, as when Boltzmann (and after him, Sommerfeld), on contemplating the great synthesizing power of Maxwell's equations that produced a panoramic unification of the fields of heat radiation, light, and electric and magnetic fields, turned to Goethe's *Faust* and quoted the line 'Was it a God who designed this hieroglyph?' [*War es ein Gott, der diese Zeichen schrieb . . .?*]

Faust's exclamation came as he opened the Book of Nostradamus and saw the Sign of the Macrocosmos. A fuller quotation goes somewhat like this:

> Was it a God designed this hieroglyph to calm
> The storm which but now raged inside me
> To pour upon my heart such balm
> And by some secret urge to guide me
> Where all the powers of Nature stand unveiled around me?
> Am I a God? It grows so light!
> .... [He contemplates the sign.]
> Into one whole how all things blend
> Function and live within each other.

Gombrich uses these passages in his discussion of 'The Paradox and the Transcendence of Language' in *Symbolic Images* (Gombrich, 1972, p. 168), and introduces it with this telling sentence: 'It is this effort to transcend the limitations of discursive speech which links the metaphor with the paradox and thus paves the way for a mystical interpretation of the enigmatic image.' This insight is applicable directly to the metaphor describing the task of the scientist that I have been developing here. It becomes rather uncanny when we read his next sentences:

> The relevant doctrine is adumbrated in Pseudo-Dionysius in a passage of crucial importance: 'The higher we rise, the more concise our language becomes, for the Intelligibles present themselves in increasingly condensed fashion. Where we shall advance into the Darkness beyond the Intelligible it will no longer be a matter of conciseness, for the words and thought cease altogether.' (Ibid.)

In the Western tradition, and chiefly in Platonic philosophy, the most exalted aims are associated with a unification and unity. 'Thus Marsilio Ficino can describe the ascent of the mind to the apprehension of the Divine as a return of the soul to its original unity . . . The ascent to unity leads to the apprehension of Beauty as an analog of the Divine.' The realms through which the soul has to rise towards God are arranged in a hierarchy — of Matter, Nature, Opinion, Reason, and Intellect — a 'hierarchy of analogies . . . The microcosm as well as the macrocosm must be envisaged as a series of concentric circles surrounding the ineffable unity in ever widening distance.' (Ibid.) In diagrammatic form we may imagine a sector, or pyramid-like slice, taken from this homocentric construction: at the bottom, at the wide part, are the regions of Matter and Nature; at the top there is convergence and unification of all lines in the point of transcendence.

It might seem that we have gone far beyond the homely metaphor of the scientist as mountaineer, clambering up with a mixture of excitement and pain, until he reaches the top, probably in a state of hyper-ventilation, and in the euphoria of self-induced narcosis generated by endomorphines in his brain. But the metaphor is much too widespread, through history and cultures, to be dismissed that easily. Rather, it is both the embodiment and the exemplification of an ambition, one which it is now not customary to speak about among scientists, but of which we can constantly overhear confessions in terms of fragments of the whole: the willingness to go to extraordinary efforts in the hope of reaching the elevation from which all puzzles before science will be resolved in one simple, coherent *Übersicht.* The exaltation that beckons is one to which a Kepler or Einstein was courageous enough to give voice openly; but it stands at least as a whispered promise before every candidate who takes part in this expedition to high ground.

This internal state of emotion of the scientist so imbued is intense. Einstein dared to say openly,

> The state of feeling which makes one capable of such achievements is akin to that of the religious worshipper or of one who is in love; his daily strivings arise from no deliberate decision or programme, but out of immediate necessity. (Trans. Holton, 1973, p. 378)

He probably embarrassed even his fellow scientists when he said so. Such passion is in striking contrast with our generally 'cool' and commonplace metaphors of the purpose of scientific work which we usually present to the public and to our beginning students. And this contrast may be significant. For a metaphor can have one of at least four purposes: to serve the individual privately; to serve the circle of the indoctrinated; to serve both of these and the more ignorant public; or to serve chiefly only the more ignorant public. Whether by necessity or not, scientists have been reserving one version of the metaphor, in this case and in many others, to themselves and their fellows, while presenting to the public another, baser version.

It is a situation familiar to anthropologists in other contexts. We must therefore add to Margaret Mead's insight on some chief sources of scientific illiteracy of the public the possibility that the wide sharing of the key metaphors is not only difficult but also not particularly encouraged. The Romantic attacks on established science seem to me motivated in part by this perception. The scientists, on the other side, can hardly help responding to the reaction in just the way they do. After all, what are they to do with the proposals of a Goethe to reorganize the study of colours and optics, when he ends his *Farbenlehre* with a section on 'Allegorical, Symbolic, Mystic Use of Colour'; he proposes that the scientists open their laboratories to other observers, to 'all natures . . . women, children'; and ends with the exhortation, the same as on the title page of Francis Bacon's *Novum Organum*: *Multi pertransibunt et augebitur scientia*. The lonely trek to the epiphaneous experience at the peak threatens to become transformed into a family outing.[3]

I end with a listing of further problems of interest to me, which I have been unable to sketch here even in sufficient outline.

(a) Categorization of metaphors.
Scientific metaphors will surely allow some categorization (those of processes versus those of structure; biological, mechanistic, technological, topological . . .). There would also appear more clearly the predominance at certain stages of historical development of certain kinds of metaphors compared to others. And synchronically, important debates between metaphoric choices will be thrown into more prominent relief.

Thus Panofsky (1956) makes the interesting point that Galileo and Kepler differed not only on the primacy of the circle for celestial mechanics. Kepler thought that 'all muscles operate according to the principle of rectilinear movement', the shifting and stretching of straight muscles in a straight line. But Galileo came to the opposite conclusion, by attending to the effect rather than the cause, to the positional change rather than muscular action; and therefore he finds himself writing that 'All human or animal movements are circular', with apparent straight-line motion being 'only secondary movements depending on the primary ones which take place at the joints' and are circular. Panofsky adds the illuminating observation that the basic contrast is really between a kinematic and a dynamic interpretation of movement, which is precisely what separated Galileo's and Kepler's astronomical notions, too.

(b) More specific tasks for the scientist as educator.
Some have been noted at several points, but I would add the explicit need for self-examination by the scientist, to become aware of the metaphoric *distance* between himself and his colleagues on the one hand and his students on the other; to be aware of the metaphoric *dissonance* that reverberates strongly, even though unattended, in every classroom. It was again Heisenberg who, in a well-known story, interrupted Felix Bloch's discourse on new ideas on the geometry of space with a remark: 'But space is blue, and birds fly in it'. The scientist needs above all watchfully to avoid

unintended or misleading but appealing metaphors. More often than not I find so-called popularizations of science shot through with the attempt to gain attention or understanding by banalized or cheapened metaphors. That is just as counterproductive with respect to scientific literacy as failing to explain the proper boundaries of the correct metaphors.

For physical scientists and to some degree biological ones, the use of *demonstrations* in the classroom — often an act of heroic effort and good intentions — can be disastrously counterproductive in terms of the transmission of the essential meaning of the phenomena. This merits special attention. Some years ago I became concerned about the question of what is conveyed by visual presentations during science lectures, and noted the almost built-in divergence between the reality of nature's phenomena experienced in the laboratory of the practising scientists, versus their carefully repackaged and media-transformed versions put before the student.

The matter is complicated by the large separation, whether by necessity or design, between experiential reality and didactic reality even when the actual phenomenon itself is shown. But it gets much worse, if as now happens more and more frequently, even the level of didactic reality is abandoned and the presenter descends to lower levels of reality: the depiction of the phenomenon by film or television; the further deterioration by presenting a machine-shop made analogon (model, animation); or, least expensive of all, a presentation of phenomena in terms of condensed coding (graph, equations, verbal narration).

In these considerations I became impressed by the function of the human presence during such demonstrations. A key observation was that many of the more successful demonstrations are actual happenings — if not on the first at least on the second level of reality, in which the *human body* is involved, as when the lecturer mounts a rotating platform to demonstrate angular momentum. To a discernible degree, such an occasion commands much added attention because the lecturer is putting his dignity and perhaps his safety at risk. A personal commitment, shown by an implicit willingness to take certain risks and evidently go to some trouble: this is the element which the participation of a human being brings that is completely lacking in the operation of the surrogates, i.e., in the presentation of a packaged and transformed metaphor, as in a film. And at the same time, another service performed by the presence of the human body alongside the actual phenomenon is to provide a *scale*, as for example in the relation of the hand to the apparatus; that, too, is usually lacking in the depiction-translation.

The scientist-educator of course negotiates easily the jump between the ground metaphor and its debased forms that actually come to the eye in the classroom. But the new student may not be able to follow him in making this leap, the more so as usually nothing is said about any necessity to make one.

Here again Gombrich has pointed to a closely related situation in his remark,

> To primitive mentality, distinction between representation and symbol is no doubt a very difficult one. Warburg described as *Denkraumverlust* this tendency of the human mind to confuse the sign with the thing signified, the name and its bearers, the literal and metaphorical, the image and its prototype . . . Our language, in fact, favours this twilight region between the literal and the metaphorical. Who can always tell where the one begins and the other ends? (Gombrich, 1972, p.125)

The scientist-educator is more likely to avoid such traps, or at least avoid the full toll, if he or she were more conscious of an *active* obligation to create lively new models, analogies, and metaphors that do not sacrifice the essential scientific content in return for easier transmission. Good writing is of course scarce in all fields; in science education it is both more needed and less frequent. The Richard Feynmans (1981) do show us that honest meaning can be preserved by writing in an engaging way, with wit and vivid style for wide audiences.

(c) Metaphor and Thema.

In what I have said, I have associated myself with *both* of two competing views of metaphor: I see metaphor acting sometimes as a means for the transfer of meaning across discontinuity, as a bridge or a boat is a means for transferring a person across a river; or, in other cases, as a more active tool of metamorphosis, of a restructuring of a portion of the world view. In either case, the metaphor has explicit or implicit boundaries. Since the metaphor is always contingent on the context, its boundary will also change as the context shifts (as it becomes possible to cut the atom, or as probabilism and indeterminacy enter).

But while the detailed shape and power of a metaphor changes, I see a constancy that endures, and that I regard as the thematic centre of the metaphor. I need only indicate here in a word or two the differences I see between metaphors and themata. Themata are near-universals of science (as they are in other cultural artefacts). They operate at the level of structure and serve to endow the successive versions of a metaphor, or a sequence of closely related metaphors, with a meaning that permits the retrieval of the inherent intention despite all evident, or even flamboyant, changes. Thus the sequence of circles, eccentrics, ellipsi, ellipsoids, precessing ellipsoids, *Ellipsenverein*, etc., are variations on one thema, namely the efficacy of geometrical explanation. In fact, as often is the case, a particular metaphor may be at the intersect of two or more themata — in this case both the efficacy of geometrical explanation and the thema of direct, centralized perception (*Anschauung*).

Science has, and always had, a mythopoeic function. The metaphor is one of the tools in that service. That does not mean it is its only function or the chief function, least of all that Dionysus is again in the saddle. Rather, it is a sign that scientific activity is, and has to be, part of a larger cultural metabolism. The scientific imagination is, after all, not the result of Special Creation. Pre-scientific and non-scientific discourse provides the proto-language of the sciences, and is in turn changed by the products of these sciences. As W.H. Letherdale has noted:

> After the capital of ordinary language had been invested by metaphor in science, the words were returned to ordinary language with the accrued interest of their scientific associations. (Letherdale, 1974, p. 242)

And Turbayne, for all his scepticism, ends by recommending a stance of cautious pragmatism:

> [Be] aware there are no proper sorts into which the facts must be allocated, but only better pictures or better metaphors. (Turbayne, 1962, p. 217)

Our scientists continue their flourishing traffic with metaphors. And our educators must also sing us new and life-sustaining ones. I feel sure the series of papers here published will help both parties to look with fresh eyes at the metaphors they use for their respective tasks. Those differ greatly in detail, but they are grounded in the same aim, an aim to which the description of Copernicus still applies: the promotion of 'the studies concerned with the most beautiful objects'.

Notes

1. I have published part of this section of the manuscript, in my *Thematic Origins of Scientific Thought* (Cambridge, Mass.: Harvard University Press), 1973, pp. 363-4.
2. All quotations from Einstein in Holton, 1979, p. 314 ff.
3. This is my own translation from G.W. Goethe, *Zur Farbenlehre*, in *Goethes Werke*, vol. XIII, pp. 522-3. Hamburg (1955; 4th edn., 1962): Christian Wegner Verlag.

Chapter Eight
Metaphors in Some Nineteenth and Twentieth-century Educational Fiction
Raymond Wilson

My concern is with fiction, a subject that has afforded educators throughout the long history of Western education with almost unlimited scope for invective and abuse. It is true that very occasionally voices have been raised maintaining the educative value of fiction, but these have usually been the voices of self-interested *littérateurs* like Coleridge or Matthew Arnold, easily drowned by the clamour of condemnation sent up by generations of heavyweight philosophers; and philosophers, we all know (not least because they themselves assure us of the fact), are dispassionate and professionally systematic thinkers, peculiarly fitted to pronounce on education.

At the head of this vilifying tradition stands Plato. In classical Greece, education was grounded in poetry and was to remain so right through the Hellenistic period, which in turn afforded the model for European higher education up to the present century. The acknowledged educator of the Greek nation was, indisputably, Homer. Even Plato cannot deny this; but as a philosopher he imagines himself (as philosophers will) to have some sort of exclusive proprietary right in matters of truth and the nature of truth. On one proposition in particular he is most insistent: that truth can be apprehended — not created, but apprehended — by the mind alone. His objection to poets, not to put too fine a point on it, is that they are liars; they are, moreover, liars who are all the more reprehensible for being first class at their job, for their fictions are both plausible and pleasurable. In short, the poet as teacher brilliantly *mis*educates. So far from awakening the mind to objectivity and truth, the 'honeyed muse' stultifies the mind, turning the pupil into a dreamer or sleepwalker by holding him in emotional thralldom to sensuous reality, which is inherently and irremediably deceptive and erroneous (Havelock, 1963).

Plato prefigures philosophic criticism down the ages when he argues that poetry miseducates, on the one hand by its fictions or erroneous content, on the other by the powerful seductiveness of its language. British philosophers, as might be expected of them, coming from a nation proverbially convinced that fine words butter no parsnips, have conspicuously held the allurements of language in contempt. Hobbes (*Leviathan*, IV) considered poetry a plaything and was venomous about 'tropes and other rhetorical figures'. Metaphor, which he designated an Abuse of Speech aimed at 'deceiving others', is accorded his particular opprobrium. Again, the committee appointed by the Royal Society in 1664 with the object of 'improving the English tongue' specifically condemns:

> This trick of *Metaphors* . . . [which] may be plac'd amongst those *general mischiefs*, such as the *dissention* of Christian Princes, the *want of practice* in Religion, and the like . . . (Spratt, 1667)

Or consider this more generalized statement of Locke from his *Essay Concerning Human Understanding*:

> . . . all the artificial and figurative application of words eloquence hath invented, are for nothing else but to insinuate wrong ideas, move the passions, and thereby mislead the judgement . . . (111, 34)

It would be easy, if tiresome, to offer more in the same vein from (say) James Mill, Jeremy Bentham, Horne Tooke, Herbert Spencer or Bertrand Russell: thinkers who share A.N. Whitehead's conviction that 'deficiencies of language stand inexorably in the way of a fundamental statement of the nature of things' (Whitehead, 1929, p. 6). If it is hardly a tribute to their logic, it is none the less a tribute to the sheer doggedness of philosophers that, from Plato to Whitehead or Richard Peters, with his slogan about 'the givenness of the world', they continue to affirm and believe in a fundamental reality that somehow, somewhere, exists outside language in general, and most certainly outside figurative or metaphoric language.

These claims, it seems to me, are contrary to all common sense, not least because the very language in which metaphor is condemned is itself a tissue of metaphor; but of metaphor that is not usually perceived to be metaphor because it is respectably dead. If a philosopher tells us that the elimination of error is a virtue, it is extremely unlikely that he is thinking of 'elimination' as an act of putting something out of doors, or of 'error' as an actual straying from the path; nor, one hopes, is he denying all possibility of 'virtue' to women, on the ground that it was, originally, manly excellence. The point I am labouring is the irony involved. Not only do philosophers have to fall back on language to argue the deficiencies of language, but they confidently proclaim the snares and deceits of metaphor, apparently unembarrassed by the fact that, necessarily, every word they use was itself once metaphor.

I myself believe that philosophers, in talking about reality, or 'the givenness of the world', are in effect doing little more than proclaiming their adherence to what has found acceptance as literal truth in language. For what is the reality, or 'givenness', even of so simple an event as an apple falling from a tree? To a pre-literate Greek, the event related to a hamadryad and a whole mythology. To a medieval schoolman, in possession of a discourse that discredited such impious fictions, the apple, being compounded of four elements, fell to earth because its predominant element was earthy. To Newton and ourselves, in possession of a newly evolved discourse of physics and mathematics, both accounts seem fanciful.

Or consider the Homeric gods, who were real enough to pre-classical Greeks. These, to Plato, were scandalously anthropomorphic fictions, but they were so because Plato was the beneficiary of recent developments in language that, in Havelock's words, achieved:

> a conversion from the image-world of the epic to the abstract world of scientific description, and from the vocabulary and syntax of narrativized events in time towards the syntax and vocabulary of equations and laws and topics which are outside time. (Havelock, 1963, p. 259)

But Plato's god, who was, of course, the latest thing in reality, and who significantly constructed matter out of beautifully proportioned right-angled triangles, and even Plato's eternally real and immutable Forms, are to modern philosophers as purely subjective and metaphoric as the Olympians he discarded; and if they are so, it is not, of course, because modern philosophers have at last pinned down reality, but because they, in their turn, confuse reality with a newly evolved scientific discourse.

They seem, in fact, to fail to learn the obvious lessons of the past, while at the same time they too often ignore the lesson of the very science they respect. For reality is surely *not* something outside us; *not* an object or 'givenness' that we as subjects neutrally observe and register. On the contrary, it is the result of an interaction between a creative intelligence and a 'givenness' that is in itself and in principle forever unknowable. What we call reality is, in short, finally an artefact. And what *kind* of artefact it is will be determined by the language or symbolism in which it is conceived, shaped and embodied. The medium may not be the message, but messages do not and cannot exist without a medium — standard English, musical or mathematical notation, the ceremony of the Mass; and whatever that medium is, it profoundly, and often uniquely and untranslatably, conditions what is said. There simply is no way of distinguishing the dancer from the dance, and our assumption that there is may well be a consequence of our speaking a European language which organizes our thinking in a subject-predicate category that does not exist in Chinese and a hundred other languages.

I have been at some trouble to try to show that statements about the nature of things, as Whitehead puts it, can never be fundamental, but are determined by the language in which they are expressed. What people say is 'true' or 'real' has no ultimate reality or truth. Homer's stories, the Bible, the Church, Ptolemaic astronomy, Newtonian physics, Marx's *Das Kapital* have all been sincerely considered repositories of truth at one time or another by intelligent people, but this only supports my contention that truth is located in the psychology of those who subscribe to it, and has no independent existence of its own. And from this it follows that however real or true our own world seems to us — every kind of world: material, social, moral, aesthetic — it is not, either in fact or principle, true or real; but will pass into the realm of what is considered fanciful or mythical or metaphorical by our successors, commensurately with their modifying or contracting or expanding those vocabularies in which what we call truth is encapsulated.

What at any particular time society at large accepts as literal in language and thinks of as objectively valid sooner or later turns out to be metaphor; but metaphor so dominant and all-pervasive as never to be recognizable as such by those held in its power. No educational theorist was ever more positive, and sincerely positive, about the purpose of education than Dickens's Mr Gradgrind in *Hard Times*, which begins in the setting of 'a plain, bare, monotonous vault of a schoolroom' that is a fitting correlative to the plain, bare, monotony of Gradgrind's deadly harangue:

> Now, what I want is, Facts. Teach these boys and girls nothing but Facts. Facts alone are wanted in life. Plant nothing else, and root out everything else. You can only form the minds of reasoning animals upon Facts: nothing else will ever be of any service to them. This is the principle on which I bring up my own children, and this is the principle on which I bring up these children. Stick to Facts, sir! (Bk. 1, Ch. I)

The confidence of Gradgrind is absolute because it is ultimately authorized by the whole development, since the Renaissance, of a scientific world-view that his society assumed to have total objectivity. Indeed, his Facts are the bricks out of which the whole vast edifice of scientific objectivity is built. For the overwhelming majority of us the edifice still stands; but for a tiny minority, capable of grasping relativity and quantum theories and the provisional and *invented* nature of scientific speculation, it crumbled at its foundations decades ago.

What *Hard Times* perhaps too insistently demonstrates is that the principle on which Gradgrind boasts he brings up his own children is disastrous. In childhood they have 'an air of jaded sullenness' resulting from an education that starves their imaginations, suppresses their natural feelings, sympathies and capacity for wonder, and removes them from all fiction and poetry likely to nourish sentiment or moral impulse. The upshot is that Tom, the son, revenges himself on his father by turning out a thief, a liar and a degenerate, while his sister, Louisa, in whom virtually all feeling is numbed, becomes a pathetically inadequate adult, sustained by Sissy Jupe, the former child of the despised circus, in whom neither Gradgrind's school nor his home, aptly named Stone Lodge, has been able to kill either a sense of fancy or the human kindness arising from it.

Hard Times is an impassioned plea on behalf of those leading lives 'of machinery and reality' for 'imaginative graces and delights, without which the heart of infancy will wither up, and the sturdiest physical manhood will be morally stark death' (Bk. 3, Ch. IX). The book has a very palpable design upon the reader and it is not hard to see why F.R. Leavis called it a 'moral fable'. However, the fabulous and fictional have not been highly regarded by British philosophers, dead or living, nor given much emphasis in our educational system, which has always been, and still is, obsessed with *cognitive* development. We have seen that Plato believed all imaginative literature to be inherently deceptive — an expression of 'opinion', deriving from the senses, never of certainty, which comes from intellectual insight. But, more sensible than so many of his successors, he was a sufficiently good Piagetian to acknowledge that children are, however regrettably, creatures of the senses, and that, as such, they must be led through poetry, the agency of the senses, towards the world of abstract thought in which truth, he imagined, is uniquely located.

Gradgrind is, of course, the beneficiary of a utilitarian, objectivistic rationalism that still profoundly moulds our Anglo-Saxon attitudes and causes us to put fiction firmly in its place, along with all those other 'tricks of metaphors' that give rise to 'general mischiefs' and all the 'figurative application of words' used to 'insinuate wrong ideas, move the passions, and thereby mislead the judgement'. In general, our historians take little

note of the evidence mere fiction affords them, and it is surely reasonable
for them to point to the dangers fiction may involve for the unwary. On the
other hand, it may be no less reasonable to admit that a good novel, by
virtue of *not* being hamstrung by the historian's factual niceties, may more
tellingly and with greater insight portray the past than a mediocre historian. One hears, however, much less about this possibility, though Aristotle
had precisely this kind of thing in mind when he spoke (*Poetics*, 7) of poetry
as something 'more philosophical and of higher value than history'. Once
more, we are brought up sharply by the pervasive positivism of the age we
live in.

I have argued there can be no ultimately objective reality and that what
we call objective reality is, properly understood, an artefact, even if it is not
recognized as such. Now I wish to advance the claim that great imaginative
literature, though recognized as an artefact, creates a 'reality' that differs
from allegedly objective reality chiefly in that it addresses itself more com-
prehensively to us, and therefore matters more. There were other voices
raised in the mid-nineteenth century against the grinding utilitarianism of
the classroom, but there is a world of difference between the abstract
criticism of a thing and the imaginative exploration and realization of it that
Hard Times gives us; and *pace* Locke, whose imaginative failure sets him
shoulder to shoulder with Gradgrind, we attain realization precisely
because 'the figurative application of words' does so successfully 'move the
passions'. A novel is nothing, if not 'the figurative application of words'; it
is, quite overtly, a metaphor, or rather, an extended and elaborated metaphor, articulated through fictive plot and character. 'A good book reads us',
and if all we find in a good novel is unreality, that can be taken as fair
comment on ourselves.

The figurative is obvious in a novel like *Hard Times*, where the opposition between fact and fancy, once established in the views advanced on
horses and flowers in the object lesson, becomes part of the story's recur-
rent symbolism. But we must never suppose an apparently realistic novel,
or apparently realistic elements within a novel, to be other than figurative.
If we turn, for instance, from elementary education to look into how the
classics fared in the nineteenth-century novel, we find a great deal of what
might pass for straightforward realism; but it would be absurdly naïve not to
recognize that the realism in a novel subserves an overall fictive purpose.

We tend to forget how exclusively pre-eminent Latin and Greek were in
middle-class education, but the 1864 Royal Commission's report on nine
Public Schools (the Clarendon Report) firmly states that 'the first, and by
far the first, matter of public instruction consisted in the two classical

languages; grammar, composition, verse-making, translation, the study of the two literatures and the committing to memory of many masterpieces'. It is noted that, except at Rugby, only classical masters were considered educators, all other masters being regarded as mere instructors. The authors of the report were less than happy, but all their strictures are milk and water compared with George Eliot's pungency in *Mill on the Floss*, published four years earlier.

Tom Tulliver, the victim of his father's well meant ambition, is sent to a clergyman tutor, Mr Stelling, who quite genuinely believes that Tom will regret not learning his supines when he grows up. Stelling, Eliot observes, is 'not the sort of man to enfeeble and emasculate his pupil's mind by simplifying and explaining', even when it is heartbreakingly obvious that 'Tom's faculties fail him before the abstractions hideously symbolized to him in the pages of the Eton grammar' (Bk. 2, Ch. 1). As an educator, Stelling has 'a favourite metaphor' — it is a metaphor that had lively acceptance throughout the last century, particularly in the Civil Service, and even now is moribund, rather than dead — namely, 'that the classics and geometry constituted that culture of the mind which prepared it for the reception of any subsequent crop'; and he is the last man to pick a quarrel with tradition when incompatibility arises between his instruction and the pupil's needs. As Eliot remarks: 'a method of education sanctioned by the long practice of our venerable ancestors was not to give way before the exceptional dullness of a boy who was merely living at the time then present.'

Torn from their contexts, such comments are not without force, but my point is that, complexly embodied in the novel, their impact is devastating. Abstract assertion, and even the liveliest polemic, cannot begin to compete with what is dramatically conceived through character, action and situation. The breathtaking unsuitability of Tom's education is not asserted, but enacted, more especially when, after his father's death, it is put to the test as a preparation for life. His Uncle Deane, one of Arnold's bourgeois philistines, and a business man, is convinced 'that if it had been good for anything, so successful a man as himself would hardly have been ignorant of it' (Bk. 3, Ch. 5). Indeed, Uncle Deane holds suspect a learning that whitens the hands and 'lies chiefly out of sight'; and his judgement is absolutely right, so far as it concerns Tom. But ironically, Tom's sister Maggie, restricted to lessons offering 'much futile information about Saxon and other kings of doubtful example', has the aptitude and intellectual hunger that might have gained a lot from the study of the classics, had not being a girl automatically precluded the mere possibility. All of which begins to add up, as all good literature does, to the kind of complexity that character-izes life itself. Basically, a novel is an extended metaphor, parading as life — but as life ordered, shaped and unified, in a way real life never is.

Towards the end of the nineteenth century, Hardy's *Jude the Obscure*, a novel often more symbolic than realistic, exposes the pending bankruptcy of classical education which, sanctified by tradition, had for centuries been regarded as the only higher education possible. The claim that the classics afford a unique and indispensable education had its origin in Renaissance literary humanism, and though the claim was taken for fact, as part of the givenness of things, its subjectiveness and inadequacy were in the end bound to be exposed by the growth of a rival scientific humanism, which also originated in the Renaissance.

As a boy, Jude first sees Oxford (Christminster) as a glimmer of lights on the horizon and mistakes it for 'the heavenly Jerusalem'. Though his aunt warns him it is 'a place much too good' for him, he swears he will force an entry, and to this end toils to educate himself, applying himself to the classical languages with the devotion of a born scholar. But Jude was in fact born a peasant, and he is to be kept out of the university by those in possession of the classical scholarship he aspires to. There is bitter irony in his being excluded from a world his talent and enthusiasm conspicuously merit by a complacent university establishment who so self-interestedly identify their scholarship (allegedly their *liberal* scholarship) with class that the idea of Jude's becoming one of them is unthinkable.

No less ironically, Hardy portrays all Jude's striving for self-education as a misapplication of effort, a turning of the mind backward to a decayed past and away from the living present, so that when Sue Bridehead tells him it is not the cathedral at Oxford, but the railway station, that is 'the centre of town life now', her unorthodoxy deeply shocks him. When first he arrives in Oxford, it is twilight: lighting up time for 'some of those lamps which sent into the sky the gleam and glory that caught his strained gaze in his days of dreaming, so many years ago.' Later that night, he explores 'the venerable city', blind to the death and decay all around him:

> When he passed objects out of harmony with the city's general expression he allowed his eyes to slip over them as if he did not see them. . . .
> Down obscure alleys, apparently never trodden now by the foot of man, and whose very existence seemed to be forgotten, there would jut into the path porticoes, oriels, doorways of enriched and florid middle-age design, their extinct air being accentuated by the rottenness of the stones. It seemed impos-sible that modern thought could house itself in such decrepit and superseded chambers. (Pt. 1, Ch. 1)

In imagination, Jude evokes the shades of dead poets, scholars, statesmen who had lived and studied there; but that is all they are — shades without substance, haunting the 'home of lost causes'.

Jude, as a stonemason, is to work, ironically enough, restoring the fabric of the university, but is never to belong to it. He is swept into the floating population infesting the sordid back-streets, and finally dies, tragically broken and alone, within earshot of the festive concert attended by 'Dons and their wives, and undergraduates with gay female companions' — the spurious outward show of an institutionalized medievalism that is 'as dead as a fernleaf in a piece of coal'.

While *Jude The Obscure* expresses an outworn tradition of education in metaphors of unfrequented alleys, phantoms and rotting masonry, it at the same time gives us the symbolic figure of Little Father Time, who hangs his siblings and himself, and about whom Hardy comments: 'Such boys are springing up among us — boys of a sort unknown in the last generation — the outcome of new views of life . . . it is the beginning of the coming universal wish not to live.' (Pt. 6, Ch. 2) We shall see the working out of Hardy's forebodings about a new type of boy when we examine *Lord of the Flies*; but first, we should look back to Golding's model for his story, R.M. Ballantyne's *The Coral Island*, published in 1858.

The Coral Island is a narrative metaphor, a fable, demonstrating how a trio of shipwrecked boys, thrown back on their own resources, and abetted by nature, fulfil a Romantic ideal. In Eden-like surroundings, away from adult influence, they ingeniously and co-operatively exploit every natural resource, 'luxuriate on the fat of the land', build and provision a boat, and generally do more than credit to Rousseau by creating a society civilized even beyond that of middle-class Victorian England!

It is doubtful whether the Victorians recognized the novel as a fable, since it so perfectly mirrors the assumptions and values of its period. In affirming progress, imperialism, self-reliance, the Creator, the goodness of nature and of human nature (when Christianized, at least), *The Coral Island* must have struck contemporary readers, who took these things for granted, as straightforwardly realistic, rather than fabulous. More than a century later, with two world wars, Belsen and Hiroshima behind us, the novel seems to us — not necessarily to our credit — embarrassingly unrealistic and phoney.

For us, the novel is a gallimaufry of high adventure, natural history and didactic moralizing, with some occasional clowning for light relief. Basically, its failure is artistic: its superficiality of plot and character are an inevitable outcome of facile writing. If one dare say so nowadays, there is nothing wrong with the sheer *decency* of the shipwrecked boys, but because this decency is unqualified and unrelated to other dimensions of character, they fail to convince and are merely emblematic. In unselfconsciously addressing one another as 'my dear boy' or 'my dear fellow', they set the tone for a novel which has, among its characteristic vocabulary, the substantives 'joy', 'wonder' and 'delight', and the adjectives 'jolly', 'cheery' and 'hearty', while much time is spent throughout in exclamatory 'Hurrahs!' over the scenery and a variety of fauna and flora. Some of this has affinities with certain kinds of progressive education, centred on discovery methods and the environment.

The moral world of the novel is no less naïve, good and evil being virtually a black-and-white issue. Evil has no place whatever in the thought, word and deed of boys who are British to the backbone. Rather, it is identified with savagery and black skin. Jack, always extraordinarily knowing, declares that 'all the natives of the South Sea Islands are fierce cannibals', and when they come to the island they very creditably live up to their reputation, slaughtering one another wholesale, eating the dead, tearing a child from its mother's arms and hurling it into the sea. Evil has invaded Paradise. However, it comes from outside. The boys are no more than witnesses and spectators of it, though, as Whitley (1970) notes, Ralph's fascination with the atrocities that keep his eyes glued upon the combatants 'could be taken to suggest a tendency towards atavism lurking *within* the characters, but . . . this remains an element which the writer either has not recognized or cannot bring himself to countenance' (p. 16).

The 'natives', meanwhile, all too visibly lack nobility and any sense of fair play in their dealings with each other. Fortunately, their natures are extremely responsive to virtue and good manners once the boys introduce them to such things, so that in the course of a morning they not only abjure cannibalism, but bury the dead and learn to shake hands like good Europeans. After this, it is no surprise to learn that 'the effect of the gospel on savage natures' turns them into honest traders; nor is it, surely, mere chance that the one native woman to have 'modesty of demeanour' and a 'gentle expression' happens to be lighter in colour than the rest. Then again, Ballantyne deftly circumvents the awkwardness presented by the pirates, who are as undeniably European as they are wicked, by calling them 'white savages'.

Were it not that Peterkin bursts into tears when Jack escapes from danger, and later half mockingly kisses Jack and Ralph on the cheek, the boys would be a credit to any Public School in Victorian England. They are unselfish, courageous, mindful of their Creator and their dear parents; they evince no impurity of language, impulse or thought and, despite their differences in age and temperament, work co-operatively for the common good. The reason Ralph gives for this is the moral centre of the entire novel:

'. . . we three on this our island, although most unlike in many things, when united, make a trio so harmonious that I question if there ever met before such an agreeable triumvirate. There was, indeed, no note of discord whatever in the symphony we played together on that sweet Coral Island; and now I am persuaded that this was owing to our having been all tuned to the same key, namely, that of *love!* Yes, we loved one another with much fervency while we lived on that island; and, for that matter, we love each other still.' (Ch. XIV)

We may not be able to avoid some post-Freudian smirking over this, but whether it is to our credit is another matter.

Now consider this passage from *Lord of the Flies*, a century later. Jack and his hunters, formerly choirboys still wearing the remains of their school caps, are about to make a kill — an act deliberately described in terms suggestive of violent sexual climax:

. . . the sow staggered her way ahead of them, bleeding and mad, and the hunters followed, wedded to her in lust, excited by the long chase and dropped blood . . . Struck down by the heat, the sow fell and the hunters hurled themselves at her. This dreadful eruption from an unknown world made her frantic; she squealed and bucked and the air was full of sweat and noise and blood and terror. Roger ran round the heap, prodding with his spear whenever pigflesh appeared. Jack was on top of the sow, stabbing downward with his knife. Roger found a lodgment for his point and began to push till he was leaning with his whole weight. The spear moved forward inch by inch and the terrified squealing became a high-pitched scream. Then Jack found the throat and the hot blood spouted over his hands. The sow collapsed under them and they were heavy and fulfilled upon her. (Golding, 1954, Ch. 8)

When 'the immediacy of the kill' subsides, Jack flicks and smears blood on the hunters, who laugh uproariously when they see that the spear has been rammed 'right up her ass!' After two of them ritually re-enact the kill, they all join in lugging out 'the hot bags of coloured guts'; then they sever the dripping sow's head and impale it on a stake and leave it in the forest as a placatory offering to 'the beast'.

Golding's boys are younger in years than Ballantyne's, but in experience older than the boys of Coral Island could ever be. Their innocence is corrupted and violated as the innocence of Ballantyne's boys is not — as Ballantyne's own essential innocence we feel is not — and what violates it is the whole world they live in: a world of atomic war. Through it they come to the island; when out of misery and fear they pray for a sign from the adult world, a dead airman falls from the sky to become the horrifying 'beast' they seek to propitiate; when they are finally saved, it is by being taken aboard a warship. But the gulf Hardy noted between generations of boys is reflected, too, in their authors' presentation. The boys of Coral Island, though they must have reached puberty, are as naïve and lacking in depth as the writing itself. The passage quoted from Golding, brief as it is, is 'knowing', as Ballantyne's language is not. Its imagery of rape and violence clings sickeningly to boys who are still some way from puberty, confirming them as inheritors of 'the Africa within'.

It is only briefly and at first that Golding's boys rejoice in being free from adults and respond to the 'glamour' of the island, and even then, their doing so is influenced by adventure stories — *Treasure Island, Swallows and Amazons, The Coral Island* — which, they discover to their cost, are wholly unrealistic idealizations of their situation. All too soon, we are aware of their post-lapsarian condition: they fail to co-operate, are thoughtless, selfish, irresponsible, deficient in practical skills, and before long dirty and afflicted with chronic diarrhoea. Sometimes Golding's irony at Ballantyne's expense is almost too obtrusive, as when Jack, who will set himself up as a merciless tribal chief, declares:

'. . . We've got to have rules and obey them. After all, we're not savages. We're English; and the English are best at everything.' (Ch. 2)

Memories of a civilization that is in ruins quickly fade. Constraints disappear as Roger, a born sadist, becomes Jack's henchman. Jack, meanwhile, successfully challenges Ralph's leadership by rejecting the authority of the conch-shell — a symbol, among other things, of democratic procedure and rational discussion — and draws to himself almost the entire group with offers of pig-flesh and a 'liberation into savagery'. Above all, he exploits the terror they all feel for a threatening 'beast', which they locate in the sea or jungle or mountain top — anywhere but where it really exists: in themselves, or more accurately in their collectivity. One boy alone, Simon, has the vision and courage to see this. He is a kind of epileptic saint-idiot, after Dostoyevsky, who becomes 'inarticulate in his effort to express mankind's essential illness', and is derided by the group. The impaled pig's head, veiled in a swarm of flies, reveals to him the truth he has been groping towards:

. . . 'You knew, didn't you? I'm part of you? Close, close, close! I'm the reason why it's no go? Why things are as they are?' (Ch. 8)

Because there is nothing left to do but to nerve himself to face truth unflinchingly, Simon climbs to the mountain top, untangles the pitiful horror of the dead airman, and makes his way in a storm back to the dark beach, where the entire group are reduced to 'the throb and stamp of a single organism' as they dance and act out a ritual slaughter to the chant of: '*Kill the beast! Cut his throat! Spill his blood!*' When Simon comes from the forest, crying out 'something about a dead man on a hill', the crowd take him for the beast and claw and tear him apart.

Ralph, the limited but essentially decent boy and elected leader of the group, is part of that crowd, as is Piggy, the brainy, unimaginative boy who stubbornly defends the adult world of 'houses an' streets an' — TV', which alone makes sense to him. When, next day, Ralph speaks of Simon's murder with 'loathing and at the same time a kind of excitement', Piggy's own limitations are highlighted. He shrilly insists it was all an accident; but his pretence of this, his fear of facing his own nature, his putting of the blame on others and even on Simon, his denial of every fact — 'We never done nothing, we never seen nothing' — and finally his plea not to 'let on we was in the dance', are a sad commentary on the humbug of the adult values he partly embodies and always upholds. Inevitably, Piggy is destroyed by Jack's savages, together with the conch-shell he cannot accept to be the fragile thing it is. Ralph, for all his limitations, has the capacity to learn through suffering, but in the end, trapped between the jungle fire and Jack's hunters, who want to impale his head on a stake, he is indistinguishable from his tormentors, 'screaming, snarling, bloody'.

Ralph's saviour, and the story's *deus ex machina*, is a naval officer, come to investigate the source of the smoke. His hand is on the butt of his revolver; behind him, in a cutter, a rating holds a sub-machine gun; behind the cutter is 'a trim cruiser' — 'trim' because ready for action. In essentials, the adult world does no more than reflect on a grander scale the island's murderous savagery. The naval officer, talking of 'fun and games' and fatuously joking ('Having a war or something?') steps straight out of Ballantyne and is literally too embarrassed for words at what he discovers:

'I should have thought,' said the officer . . . 'I should have thought that a pack of British boys — you're all British aren't you? — would have been able to put up a better show than that — I mean . . .'

Ralph breaks down and cries and:

. . . infected by that emotion, the other little boys [hunters and killers a minute ago] began to shake and sob too. And in the middle of them, with filthy body, matted hair, and unwiped nose, Ralph wept for the end of innocence, the darkness of man's heart . . . (Ch. 12)

The Coral Island and *Lord of the Flies* are both metaphors of the human condition. The first is optimistic, innocent, committed to knowledge and progress and secure in the faith that man's nature tends to goodness as water flows downhill. The second is pessimistic, darkened by experience, sceptical about both knowledge and progress and tragic in its acceptance of man's fallen nature and inclination to evil.

Clearly, these metaphors relate very much to their periods. What I find extraordinary about Anglo-Saxon educational philosophy is that it so manifestly belongs to the naïve world of Coral Island in its unreflecting assumptions about the worthwhileness of knowledge and, in particular, about the worthwhileness of just those paradigm forms of knowledge which in Golding's fable lead to a world in ruins. Ballantyne's Jack is several times called a philosopher and certainly his deft exclusion from consideration of whatever disturbs his prejudice in favour of a rational universe still serves as a model for his twentieth-century successors:

. . . 'I never saw a ghost myself, and I never met with anyone who had; and I have generally found that strange and unaccountable things have almost always been accounted for, and found to be quite simple, on close examination.' (Ch. VIII)

Whatever cannot be so accounted for — say, 'the darkness of man's heart' — can safely be said not to exist or not to have meaning. To millions of students in five continents, among whom it has become a cult book, *Lord of the Flies* speaks with all the authenticity of a great poem. Notoriously, poetry cannot be translated; and this, of course, is why Golding's metaphor is ignored by our educational philosophers. Like Ballantyne's Jack, they are dismissive for whatever is too complex or subtle to be reductively restated in an impoverished, philosophic prose, and their psychological security depends on their having everything on *their* terms.

In Golding's fable we are constantly aware of forces destructive of humanity, whether they are technological and derive from the intellect, or an inheritance from our animal past. Among its manifold meanings, the story gives us a vivid insight into what Koestler sees abstractly as 'evolutionary error': that is, an incongruity between the recently evolved human neocortex and the uncoordinated archaic and reptilian structure of our brains. Aldous Huxley's *Brave New World* (1931) offers, by way of metaphor, a resolution of the problem for all time.

Among the inhabitants of *Brave New World* no incongruity is permitted to exist between neocortex and animal impulse. Any such incongruity would be unthinkable — literally so — in a world that realizes the philosopher's dream of achieving the happiness of its entire population by the most rigorous application of science and rational principle. All you need is, first, a 'foolproof system of eugenics, designed to standardize the human product' for whichever social and occupational function it is intended; second, you need certain perfected Skinnerian conditioning techniques; third, you need to ensure that the human product's conditioned expectations are throughout life exactly matched and provided for. If these conditions are met, as they are in Huxley's satire, you are left with New World citizens who are *necessarily* happy and who *cannot but* live in harmony with society and themselves. All they have lost in the process is individuality or the painful privilege of being truly human; but then again, their conditioning precludes their awareness of this.

All serious science fiction projects features of existing society onto the large screen of the future. Needless to say, the enlargement shows up for our examination every flaw in what is projected, and notoriously authors have underestimated the time needed for their fiction to be outstripped by fact. In his 1946 foreword to *Brave New World* Huxley himself comments:

> All things considered, it looks as though Utopia were far closer to us than anyone, only fifteen years ago, could have imagined. Then, I projected it six hundred years into the future. Today it seems quite possible that the horror may be upon us within a single century.

As a measure of how far we have moved since then, we might reflect on our test-tube babies and developments in cloning and in molecular biology. As long ago as 1966, Nobel prizewinner Sir Macfarlane Burnet gave up his research, announcing: 'So far as the advance of medicine is concerned, molecular biology is an evil thing.' Quite specifically, he feared that research, having the potential to remould human beings intellectually and emotionally by tampering with genetic systems, could lead to the horror Huxley predicts. However, Maurice Wilkins (1966), Professor of Molecular Biology at London University, spoke for the scientific fraternity — and, so far as I know, for educationists generally, since they might be supposed to have a very real stake in all this — in expressing the healthy, extravert view that the whole matter was 'largely trivial' and must not be used 'as an excuse' for holding up research.

Of course, research was not held up, though one suspects much of it is now hushed up. 'Progress *is* lovely' continues to be a hypnopaedic truism even in the stasis of the Brave New World. Meanwhile, Huxley's metaphors are quickly catching up on us. If we have not yet progressed to the point of destroying the family and enforcing promiscuity, we have at least handed over to the Welfare State many of the family's traditional responsibilities, legally sanctioned serial polygamy by easing divorce and actually set up the prophesied Abortion Centres. If we do not yet have Re-conditioning Centres, we do have Rehabilitation Centres; if not hypnopaedia, then massively researched hidden persuasion; if not feelies, then pornographic cinema; and if not *soma*, then a whole pharmacopoeia of stimulants and drugs. For the vast majority of us, God *is* incompatible with machines and science, and the past and its values are in practice assumed to be outgrown — not least in education, where there is overriding concern for immediacy and 'relevance'.

The Brave New World has chosen, as its highest priority, universal happiness. Everything in its organization follows logically from this. The entire population is so programmed as to pursue 'self-indulgence up to the very limit imposed by hygiene and economics'. Programming is, of course, a negation of individuality; but as the Director asks, gesturing towards rows of microscopes, test-tubes and incubators, '. . . after all, what is an individual?' Standard individuals, whether Alphas or Epsilons, can be mass-produced indefinitely, their production being limited only by the need to preserve the balance necessary to maximizing happiness within the total population. Individuals are so many cells, contributory to the health and happy functioning of the social body. As such, they have no rights, not even to privacy, but always identify with the crowd that Kierkegaard labels 'the untruth'. They are *compulsorily* virtuous and content, for, as the Controller says:

> '. . . they get what they want, and they never want what they can't get. They're well off; they're safe; they're never ill; they're not afraid of death; they're blissfully ignorant of passion and old age; they're plagued with no mothers or fathers; they've got no wives, or children, or loves to feel strongly about; they're so conditioned that they practically can't help behaving as they ought to behave. And if anything should go wrong, there's *soma*.' (Ch. XVI)

There is irony in this triumph of science, since by achieving lasting stability for society, it at the same time cuts off all possibility of its own future development. The values and logic that obtained at the time of its triumph are thenceforth perpetuated in a *huis clos*. When occasionally the conditioning of Alphas is not quite absolute, as happens with Bernard and Helmholtz, the system has means for removing such irritants to where they can do no harm. The single character with whom we can identify is John, the Savage from an Indian reservation. Because he is the son of a 'civilized' mother, he has grown up an outsider, under the influence of 'a religion that is half fertility cult and half *Penitente* ferocity' and a chance copy of Shakespeare, whose work is unknown in the civilized world, except to the Controller. John has individuality, a half-articulate appreciation of tragedy and high art, together with the heroic values they affirm, and pride in his personal freedom. The Controller fails to persuade him that contentment counts for more than tragedy, which derives from social instability, or that high art is worth sacrificing for the sake of the unspectacular happiness stability guarantees.

What the Controller argues for is a world sterilized of unpleasantness and pain: a beautiful, if necessarily unheroic, world. The cost is too little for John, who knows that beauty can only be bought with tears and that nothing worth anything can ever be exempt from risk and suffering. Even here the Controller has an answer:

> 'Violent Passion Surrogate. Regularly once a month. We flood the whole system with adrenin. It's the complete physiological equivalent of fear and rage. All the tonic effects of murdering Desdemona and being murdered by Othello, without any of the inconveniences.'
> 'But I like the inconveniences.'
> 'We don't,' said the Controller. 'We prefer to do things comfortably.'
> 'But I don't want comfort. I want God, I want poetry, I want real danger, I want freedom, I want goodness. I want sin.'
> 'In fact,' said Mustapha Mond, 'you're claiming the right to be unhappy.'
> 'All right, then,' said the Savage defiantly, 'I'm claiming the right to be unhappy.'
> 'Not to mention the right to grow old and ugly and impotent; the right to have syphilis and cancer; the right to have too little to eat; the right to be lousy; the right to live in constant apprehension of what may happen tomorrow; the right to catch typhoid; the right to be tortured by unspeakable pains of every kind.'
> There was a long silence.
> 'I claim them all,' said the Savage at last. (Ch. XVI)

And indeed he claims *more*. Tortured by his love for Lenina, whose education ensures that love means nothing more than promiscuous sex, he seeks penitential solitude, only to be hounded by sightseers and newsmen. Rather than come to terms with their defiling civilization, he takes his own life.

Huxley's fable is a bitter satire on the materialism of twentieth century consumer society and its attendant science and technology. Man, by using his reason to attain the ultimate life of pleasure, ceases to be man. In *Lord of the Flies*, the boys have to hide behind paint before they can abase themselves in savagery. In *Brave New World* man's abasement is blandly accomplished behind a camouflage of scientific and technological progress. And it is *precisely* scientific and technological progress that every country in the world — capitalist or communist, developed or developing — is, if I may use a Faustian metaphor, hell-bent on pursuing. Though they may argue about means, it is the one end that all governments and opposition parties are entirely agreed upon, and require their systems of education to adjust to and subserve.

Hardy, in his ironic and tragic exposition, through Jude, of the breakdown of classical-Christian tradition, recognized clearly enough that 'new views on life,' deriving from a morally vacuous world view, must usher in the coming universal deathwish. Yeats, too, saw the madness and chaos that must ensue:

> You ask what makes me sigh, old friend,
> What makes me shudder so?
> I shudder and I sigh to think
> That even Cicero
> And many-minded Homer were
> *Mad as the mist and snow.*

It is nowadays a fashion, and nowhere more so than among educators, not simply to genuflect before the rigour and creative and imaginative challenges of science, but to pretend that science is wholly compatible with, if not actually promotive of, religion, values and the arts. However, the classical-Christian tradition in education did not collapse under its own weight, but under the intolerable pressure brought to bear on it by a *displacing* scientific outlook. Today, the displacement shows itself as unmistakably in the curriculum as it does in a defunct church advertising bingo. Nor is it a straightforward matter of the sciences establishing and expanding their position: they at the same time usurp so much prestige that the arts lose confidence and even seek salvation by absurdly aping them.

Here, briefly, are some quotations from *Crisis in the Humanities* (Plumb, 1964). Professor Finley, defending the classics:

> The study of Latin can help with the study and use of English . . . And perhaps a little grinding discipline is a good thing at the schoolboy age anyway . . . No case can be made for Latin . . . on the ground that its study will help prevent 'loose thought and careless speech' . . . (p. 18)

Professor Plumb, defending history:

This century has witnessed 'the brilliant conquest of the most distant frontiers of historical knowledge', yet fewer and fewer historians believe that their art has any social purpose . . . (p. 25)

Professor Hough on literary education:

One cannot be very exhilarated by an outlook that consists mainly of automatic negations and routine nonconformities. And far too often that is all that a literary education has to offer. (p. 96)

Professor Vidler on divinity:

Professional theologians . . . never seem to have any devastating new ideas, at least not ones that they succeed in communicating outside their own coterie. Not until something of this sort happens will 'divinity' once more make a lively impact in the field of higher education . . . (p. 95)

With apologists like this, we have no need of detractors. But where, outside the humanities themselves, can our humanity be given definition and direction? All the smooth talk about the exact balance of forms of knowledge put forward by our curriculum theorists and planners fails so much as to grasp, let alone solve, the basic problem of our age, which is to know what values can be brought to bear on the exponential growth of science, when the development of science unavoidably discredits and discards values. Huxley's Brave New World is one logical outcome of the uncontrolled developments in science. So, too, in the shorter term, is Golding's fable, the savagery and atavism of which have their analogue in the violence, terrorism and disorder of our own society, while in the background of the story, as in the background of all our thinking and feeling, is an atomic war.

'What's the point of truth or beauty or knowledge,' Huxley's Controller asks, 'when the anthrax bombs are popping all around?' He would be kept an unconscionable time waiting, if he wanted an answer from our educationists and philosophers, who seem to feel that all discussion of substantive issues is some kind of indiscretion. Whether knowledge really is an automatic good, whether science is controllable and if so, how and by whom, and whether technological development is compatible with human development, or even human survival, are questions too large, too near the bone and, above all, too uncomfortable to positivistic assumptions to merit their attention. Half-educated as he is, Huxley's Savage is not far out in defining a philosopher as 'a man who dreams of fewer things than there are in heaven and earth.'

Gradgrind's scientifically objective universe is still the dominant myth of Western man, who mistakes it for actuality. In the same field as Sir Macfarlane Burnet, though utterly opposed to his views, is the celebrated author of *Chance and Necessity* (1972), Jacques Monod. Whatever might be said against him, Monod at least confronts real issues, and does so with all the confidence and directness of Gradgrind himself. He is, in fact, Gradgrind with a Nobel prize. All mankind has to do, he insists, is to make objectivity 'the *conditio sine qua non* of true knowledge'. This knowledge will then be 'exclusive of all value judgement (except that of "epistemological value")' and it will enable humankind to jettison the whole of what we now call our values as so much error, inherited from our deluded ancestors. For the source of truth and moral inspiration, Monod declares, can exist only:

> ... in the sources of science itself, in the ethic upon which knowledge is founded, and which by free choice makes knowledge the supreme value — the measure and guarantee for all other values. (p. 166)

It is sad that we have no Dickens to satirize this Knowledge Ethic, in which our Anglo-Saxon philosophic tradition is grounded, implicitly at least. Not that novels need to be taken at all seriously, of course. After all, they are no more than fiction, fancy, fables — mere eloquent metaphors on our human condition, and as such fit 'for nothing else but to insinuate wrong ideas, move the passions, and thereby mislead the judgement'.

References

ACKERMAN, M.B. (1980), *Social Justice and the Liberal State*. New Haven, Conn.: Yale University Press.

ADAMS, Sir J. (1912), *The Evolution of Educational Theory*. London: Macmillan.

ALSTON, W.P. (1964), *Philosophy of Language*. Englewood-Cliffs, N. J.: Prentice-Hall.

ARENDT, H. (1963), quoted in Bollinger (1980), p. 143; from the *American Scholar*, 32, p. 532.

—— (1978), *The Life of the Mind. Vol. 1: Thinking*. London: Secker and Warburg.

AUSKI, P. (1975), 'Wyclif's sermons and the plain style.' *Archives for Reformation History*, 66, pp. 5–23.

AUSTIN, J.L. (1962), *How to do Things with Words* (ed. J.O. Urmston). Oxford: Clarendon Press.

AUSTIN, M. (1971), 'Dream recall and the bias of intellectual ability.' *Nature*, 231.

AYER, A.J. (1946), *Language, Truth and Logic*. London: Gollancz (2nd. edn.).

BATESON, G. (1973), *Steps to an Ecology of Mind*. London: Paladin.

—— (1980), *Mind and Nature: A necessary unity*. New York: Bantam Books.

BAYLEY, L. (1612), *The Practice of Pietie*.

BENFEY, O.T. (1982), 'Chemistry — mechanical, organicist, or magical?' *Journal of Chemical Education*, May.

BENJAMIN, H. (1971), 'The sabre-tooth curriculum' in Hooper, R. (ed), *The Curriculum*. Edinburgh: Oliver and Boyd.

BLACK, M. (1962), *Models and Metaphors*. Ithaca, N.Y.: Cornell University Press.

—— (1977a), 'more about metaphor', *Dialectica* 31(3-4) (repr. in Ortony, A. (ed.), 1979).

—— (1977b), 'How metaphors work: a reply to Donald Davidson' in Sacks S. (ed.) (1979)

BLOOM, B.S. (ed.) (1956), *The Taxonomy of Educational Objectives 1: Cognitive Domain.* London: Longman.

BOBBITT, F. (1918), *The Curriculum.* New York: Houghton Mifflin.

BÖHME, G. (1981), 'Towards a reconstruction of Kant's epistemology and theory of science.' *The Philosophical Forum,* 13 (1), Fall.

BOLLINGER, D. (1980), *Language — The Loaded Weapon.* London: Longman.

BOURDIEU, P. (1977), *Reproduction in Education, Society and Culture.* London: Sage Publications.

BORN, L.K. (1936), Translation of Erasmus, *Education of a Christian Prince* (1516). New York: Columbia University Press.

BOWLES, S. and GINTIS, H. (1976), *Schooling in Capitalist America.* New York: Basic Books. (London: Routledge and Kegan Paul.)

—— (1980), 'Contradiction and reproduction in educational theory' in Barton, L. et al., *Schooling, Ideology and the Curriculum.* Brighton: Falmer Press.

BOYD, R. (1979), 'Metaphor and theory change' in Ortony, A. (ed.)

BRUSH, S.G. (1981), 'Theories of the origin of the solar system 1900-1960' in Hanle, P.A. and Chamberlin, Von Dell (eds.), *Space Science Comes of Age.* Washington: Smithsonian Institute Press.

BULLOCK, A. and STALLYBRASS, O. (eds.) (1977), *The Fontana Dictionary of Modern Thought.* London: Collins. (*The Harper Dictionary of Modern Thought.* New York: Harper and Row.)

BURKE, K. (1945), *A Grammar of Motives.* New York: Prentice Hall.

BUTOR, M. (1971), 'The novel as research' in Bradbury, M. (ed.), *The Novel Today.* London: Fontana.

CANNON, C.K. (1962), 'William Whitaker's *Disputatio de Sacra Scriptura* (1588): a sixteenth-century theory of allegory.' *Huntington Library Quarterly,* XXV, pp. 129-38.

CAPLAN, H. (1929), 'The four senses of scriptural interpretation and the medieval theory of preaching.' *Speculum,* 4, pp. 282-90.

CASSIRER, E. (1925), *Philosophie der Symbolischen Formen.* Berlin: B. Cassirer.

—— (1953), *Language and Myth.* New York: Dover.

CHAPMAN, G. (1595), *Ovid's Banquet of Sence.*

CHOMSKY, N. (1965), *Aspects of the Theory of Syntax.* Cambridge, Mass.: M.I.T. Press.

CLARK, E. and CLARK, H. (1978), 'Universals, relativity and language processing' in Greenberg, J.H., *Universals of Human Language*. Vol. 1: *Method and Theory*, pp. 225–77. Stanford, Calif.: Stanford University Press.

COHEN, D. (1979), 'Psychological novels' in *American Psychological Association Monitor*, November, p. 10.

COHEN, T. (1979), 'Metaphor and the cultivation of intimacy' in Sacks, S. (ed.).

COHEN, J. (1981), *The Lineaments of Mind: In historical perspective*. London: Freeman.

COOPER, D.E. (1972), 'Searle on intentions and reference.' *Analysis*, 32, pp. 159–63.

—— (1973), *Philosophy and the Nature of Language*. London: Longman

COPERNICUS, N. (c. 1530, trans. E. Rosen 1978), *De Revolutionibus Orbium Coelestium*. Baltimore, Md.: John Hopkins University Press.

CURTIUS, E.R. (1953), *European Literature and the Latin Middle Ages*. London: Routledge and Kegan Paul.

D'ANGELO, F.J. (1971), *A Conceptual Theory of Rhetoric*. Cambridge, Mass.: Winthrop.

DARLING, J. (1982), 'Education as horticulture: growth theories and their critics.' *Journal of Philosophy of Education* 16(2), pp. 173–85.

DAVIDSON, D. (1978), 'What metaphors mean.' *Critical Enquiry*, 5, Autumn 1978, pp. 31–47, repr. in Sacks, S. (1979), and in Platts, M. de B. (1980).

DEARDEN, R.F. (1968), *The Philosophy of Primary Education*. London: Routledge and Kegan Paul.

—— (1975), 'Education as a process of growth' in Dearden R.F., Hirst, P.H. and Peters, R.S. (eds.), *Education and the Development of Reason*. London: Routledge and Kegan Paul.

—— (1981), 'Balance and coherence: some curricular principles in recent reports.' *Cambridge Journal of Education*, II (2).

DERRIDA, J. (1978), *Writing and Difference* (trans. with an introduction and additional notes by Bass, A.). London: Routledge and Kegan Paul.

D.E.S. (Department of Education and Science) (1980), *Framework for the School Curriculum*. London: HMSO.

DEUTSCH, M. (1958), 'Evidence and inference in nuclear research.' *Daedalus*, 87, Fall.

DEWEY, J. (1938), *Logic: The theory of enquiry*. New York: Henry Holt.

DUPUY, J.P. (1980), 'Myths of informational society' in Woodward K. (ed.),

The Myths of Information: Technology and post-industrial culture. London: Routledge and Kegan Paul.

EARLE, J. (1628), *Microcosmographie.*

EDEL, A. (1973), 'Analytic philosophy of education at the crossroads' in Doyle, J.F. (ed.), *Educational Judgements.* London: Routledge and Kegan Paul, pp. 242–3.

EDWARDS, A. (1980), 'Schooling for change: function, correspondence and cause' in Barton, L., Meigham, R. and Walter, S. *Schooling, Ideology and the Curriculum.* Brighton: Falmer Press.

EINSTEIN, A. (1933), *On the Method of Theoretical Physics.* Oxford: Clarendon Press.

—— (1936), 'Physics and reality.' *Journal of the Franklin Institute,* 221, pp. 349–82.

EISNER, E.W. (1969), 'Instructional and expressive objectives' in Popham, W.J. et al.

EMPSON, W. (1930), *Seven Types of Ambiguity.* London: Chatto and Windus.

ENTWISTLE, H. (1970), *Child-centred Education.* London: Methuen.

—— (1979), *Antonio Gramsci: Conservative schooling.* London: Routledge and Kegan Paul.

FEYNMAN, R. (1981), 'Challenger lectures.' *Project Physics Course Text* (3rd edn.). New York: Holt, Rinehart and Winston.

FITZGERALD, W. (1849), Translation of William Whitaker's *A Disputation on Holy Scripture.* Cambridge: Parker Society.

FRAME, D.M. (1958), Translation of 'The education of children' in *The Complete Works of Montaigne.* London: Hamish Hamilton.

FREIRE, P. (1971), *Pedagogy of the Oppressed.* London: Penguin.

GALLIE, W.B. (1955), 'Essentially contested concepts.' *Proceedings of the Aristotelian Society,* 56.

—— (1956), 'Art as essentially contested concept.' *Philosophical Quarterly,* 6.

GARDINER, S.R. (1898), *History of the Great Civil War.* London: Longman.

GASS, W. (1976), *On Being Blue.* Boston, Mass.: Godine.

GEERTZ, C. (1980), 'Blurred genres.' *American Scholar,* 49.

GELLNER, E. (1959), *Words and Things.* London: Gollancz.

GILES, J.A. (ed.) (1864), *The Whole Works of Roger Ascham,* III. London: J.R. Smith.

GOLDING, W. (1954), *Lord of the Flies.* London: Faber and Faber.

GOMBRICH, E.H. (1970), *Aby Warburg: An intellectual biography.* London: The Warburg Institute.

—— (1972), *Symbolic Images: Studies in the art of the Renaissance.* London: Phaidon.

—— (1978), *Ideals and Idols*. Oxford: Phaidon.

GOODMAN, N. (1968), *Languages of Art: An approach to a theory of symbols*. Indianapolis: Bobbs-Merrill.

—— (1979), 'Metaphor as moonlighting.' in Sacks, S. (1979).

HAKE, E. (1574), *A Touchstone for Time Present*.

HARDIE, C.D. (1942), *Truth and Fallacy in Educational Theory*. Cambridge: The University Press. (Repr. 1962, Columbia, New York: Teachers College Press.)

HARDING, T. (ed.) (1849), Heinrich Bullinger's *Decades*. Cambridge: Parker Society.

HARRISON, B. (1979), *An Introduction to the Philosophy of Language*. London: Macmillan.

HARRISON, J.E. (1963). *Themis, A Study in the Social Origin of Greek Religion*. London: Merlin Press.

HAVELOCK, E.A. (1963), *Preface to Plato*. Oxford: Basil Blackwell.

HAWKES, T. (1972), *Metaphor*. London: Methuen.

HAWKINS, M.J. (ed.) (1972), *Essays of Francis Bacon*. London: Dent.

HEIDEGGER, M. (1971), *Erläuterungen zu Hölderlins Dichtung*. Frankfurt am Main: Klostermann (4th edn.).

HEILBRON, J.L. (1981), 'Rutherford-Bohr atom.' *American Journal of Physics*, 49, March.

HERFORD, C.H. (1945), *Timber or Discoveries* (1641) in *Ben Jonson: Works*, *VIII*. Oxford: Clarendon Press.

HILL, C. (1967), *Reformation to Industrial Revolution*. London: Penguin.

HIRST, P.H. (1972), 'The nature of educational theory: reply to D.J. O'Connor.' *Proceedings of the Philosophy of Education Society of Great Britain*, 6(1).

HOARE, Q. (ed.) (1977), *Gramsci: Selections from the Political Writings 1910-20*. New York: International Publishers.

—— and SMITH, G.N. (eds.) (1971), *Gramsci: Selections from the Prison Notebooks*. London: Lawrence and Wishart.

HOLTON, G. (1965), 'Conveying science by visual presentation' in Kepes, G. *Education of Vision*. New York: George Braziller.

—— (1973), *Thematic Origins of Scientific Thought*. Cambridge, Mass.: Harvard University Press.

—— (1978), *The Scientific Imagination: Case Studies*. Cambridge: The University Press.

—— (1979), 'Constructing a theory: Einstein's model.' *American Scholar*, 48(3), Summer, pp. 309-40.

—— (1981) 'Einstein's search for the *Weltbild*' *Proceedings of the American Philosophical Society*, 125(1), February.

HUDSON, L. (1968), *Frames of Mind.* London: Methuen.

—— (1972), *The Cult of the Fact.* London: Cape.

—— (1978), *The Nympholepts.* London: Cape.

—— (1982), *Bodies of Knowledge.* London: Weidenfeld and Nicholson.

HUXLEY, A. (1931), *Brave New World.* London: Chatto and Windus.

JAMES, C. (1968), *Young Lives at Stake.* London: Collins.

KANT, I. (1960), *Religion within the Limits of Reason Alone.* New York: Harper.

KERMODE, F. (1977), 'Can we say absolutely anything we like?' in Anderson, Q., Donadio, S. and Marcus, S. (eds.), *Art, Politics and Will: Essays in honour of Lionel Trilling.* New York: Basic Books.

KINNEAVY, J.L. (1971), *A Theory of Discourse.* Englewood Cliffs, N.Y.: Prentice-Hall.

KNORR, K.D. (1980), 'The scientist as an analogical reasoner: A critique of the metaphor theory of innovation' in Knorr, K.D., Krohn, R. and Whitley, R. (eds.), *The Social Process of Scientific Investigation.* Holland: D. Reidel Publishing

KNOTT, B.I. (1978), Translation of Erasmus *De Copia* in *Complete Works in English,* 24. Toronto: University of Toronto Press.

KOMISAR, B.P. (1961), ' "Need" and the "Needs curriculum" ' in Othanel Smith, B. and Ennis, R.H. (eds.), *Language and Concepts in Education.* Chicago: Rand McNally.

LAKOFF, G. and JOHNSON, M. (1980), *Metaphors We Live By.* Chicago: University of Chicago Press.

Language Department of the School of Economic Science (1975), *The Letters of Marsilio Ficino* translated from the Latin by members of the School of Economic Science, London London: Shepheard-Walwyn.

LAPORTE, P.M. (1966), 'Cubism and Relativity, with a letter of Albert Einstein.' *Art Journal,* 25(3).

LAWNER, L. (ed.) (1979), *Gramsci: Letters from Prison.* London: Quartet Books.

LECHNER, E. (1912), *Physikalische Weltbilder.* Leipzig: Theodore Thomas Verlag.

LEHMBERG, S.E. (ed.) (1962), *The Boke Named The Governour* by Thomas Elyot. London: Dent.

LESSING, D. (1972), 'Not a very nice story' in *The Temptation of Jack Orkney and Other Stories.* New York: Knopf. London: Cape.

LESSINGER, L.M. and TYLER, R.W. (eds.) (1971), *Accountability in Education.* Washington D C: Jones.

LETHERDALE, W.H. (1974), *The Role of Analogy, Model and Metaphor in*

Science. New York: American Elsivir Publishing Co.

LOCKE, J. (1731), *An Abridgement of Mr Locke's Essay Concerning Human Understanding* (4th edn.). London: J Knapton.

LOCKYER, K.G. (1974), *Factory and Production Management.* London: Pitman.

LOGAN, P. (1981), 'Language and Physics.' *Physics Education,* 16, pp. 174–7.

LUKES, S. (1977), 'Some problems about rationality' in Wilson, B.R. (ed.), *Rationality.* Oxford: Basil Blackwell, pp. 194–213.

MacDONALD, B. (1978), 'Accountability, standards and the process of schooling' in Becher, T. and Maclure, S., *Accountability in Education.* Windsor: NFER Publishing.

MacGREGOR, B. (1978), Translation of Erasmus *De Ratione* (1511) in *Complete Works in English,* 24. Toronto: University of Toronto Press.

MacNEICE, L. and STAHL, E.L. (trans.) (1965), Goethe's *Faust.* London: Faber.

MacRAE, D.G. (1975), 'The body and social metaphor' in Benthall, J. and Polhemus, T., *The Body as a Medium of Expression.* London: Allen Lane.

MACH, E. (1943), *Popular Scientific Lectures.* LaSalle Ill: Open Court.

MAGER, R.F. (1962), *Preparing Instructional Objectives.* Palo Alto: Fearon.

MAILER, N. (1974), *Marilyn.* New York: Grosset and Dunlop.

MAYER, A.M. (1878), *Silliman's American Journal,* April 1878; reprinted in *Phil Mag.*

McCARTHY, M. (1957), *The Company She Keeps.* London: Weidenfeld and Nicholson.

—— (1963), Interviews in *Writers at Work* (2nd series); introduced by Brooks, V.W. London: Secker and Warburg.

McNAMARA, D.M. (1981), 'Attention, time on task and children's learning: research or ideology?' in *Journal of Education for Teaching,* 7(3), Oct.

MEAD, M. (1959), 'Closing the gap between the scientists and the others.' *Daedalus,* 88, pp. 139–46.

MEDLEY, D.M. (1979), 'The effectiveness of teachers' in Peterson, P.L. and Walberg, H.J. (eds.), *Research on Teaching.* Berkeley, Calif.: McCutchan.

MEREDITH, J.C. (ed.) (1952), Immanuel Kant's *Critique of Judgement.* London: Oxford University Press.

MIDGLEY, M. (1980), 'Gene-juggling' in Montague, M.J.A. (ed.), *Sociobiology Examined.* Oxford: Oxford University Press.

MILLER, A.I. (1978), 'Visualization lost and regained: the genesis of the Quantum Theory in the period 1913–1927' in Wechsler J. (ed.), *On Aesthetics in Science.* Cambridge, Mass.: M.I.T. Press.

—— (1983), 'Redefining *Anschaulichkeit*' in Shimony. A. and Feshbach, H. (eds.), *Physics as Natural Philosophy: A festschrift for Laszlo Tisza*. Cambridge, Mass.: M.I.T. Press.

MONOD, J. (1972), *Chance and Necessity*. London: Collins.

MYNORS, R.A.B. (1978), trans. of Erasmus, *Parabolae* (1511), Dedicatory Letter to Pieter Gillis in *Complete Works in English*, 23. Toronto: University of Toronto Press.

NASH, P. (1981), 'Connection and separation: Bateson's double bind.' *Journal of Applied Behavioural Science*, 17(3).

NEALE, J.E. (1973), *Queen Elizabeth I*. London: Penguin.

OAKESHOTT, M. (1975), 'Education: the engagement and its frustration' in Dearden, R.F. Hirst, P.H. and Peters, R.S., *Education and the Development of Reason*. London: Routledge and Kegan Paul.

—— quoted BURGIN K. (1981), 'The poverty of political science' in *New Universities Quarterly*, Autumn.

O'CONNOR, D.J. (1957), *An Introduction to the Philosophy of Education*. London: Routledge and Kegan Paul.

ORTONY, A. (ed.) (1979), *Metaphor and Thought*. Cambridge: The University Press.

PALFREYMAN, T. (1567), *A Treatise on Morall Philosophy*.

PANOFSKY, E. (1956), 'Galileo as a critic of the arts: aesthetic attitude and scientific thought.' *ISIS*, 47, pp. 3–15.

PARLETT, M.R. and HAMILTON, D. (1976), 'Evaluation as illumination' in Towney, D. (ed.), *Evaluation Today*. London: Macmillan.

PASSMORE, J. (1966), *A Hundred Years of Philosophy*. New York: Basic Books.

PATTERSON, F.A. (ed.) (1931–40), Milton's *Of Education* (1644) *Prolusion VII* and *Apology for Smectymnuus* (1642) in *The Works of John Milton*. New York: Columbia University Press.

PEPPER, S. (1948), *World Hypotheses*. Berkeley, Calif.: University of California Press.

PETERS, R.S. (1964), *Education as Initiation* (Inaugural Lecture, 9 December 1963). London: University of London Institute of Education.

—— (1965), 'Education as initiation' in Archambault, R. (ed.), *Philosophical Analysis and Education*. London: Routledge and Kegan Paul, pp. 87–111.

PICKERING, A. (1980), 'Exemplars and analogies.' *Social Studies of Science*, 10, pp. 497–508.

PLATTS, M. de. B. (1980), *Reference, Truth and Reality*. London: Routledge and Kegan Paul.

PLOWDEN REPORT (1967), *Children and Their Primary Schools*. London: HMSO.

PLUMB, J.H. (1964), *Crisis in the Humanities*. London: Penguin.

POPHAM, W.J. et al. (1969), *Industrial Objectives*. American Educational Research Association, Monograph 3. Chicago: Rand McNally.

POPPER, K.R. (1972), *Objective Knowledge*. Oxford: Clarendon Press.

QUINE, W.V. (1979), 'A postscript on metaphor' in Sacks, S. (ed.).

RICHARDS, I.A. (1950), *The Philosophy of Rhetoric*. New York: Oxford University Press.

RICOEUR, P. (1978), *The Rule of Metaphor: Multi-disciplinary studies of the creation of meaning in language* (trans. Czerny, R.). London: Routledge and Kegan Paul.

ROBINSON, J. (1979), 'Introduction' to Walsh, V. and Fram, H., *Classical and Neoclassical Theories of Equilibrium* (Oxford) quoted by R.L. Heilbroner in a review of A.S. Eichner, *A Guide to Post-Keynesian Economics* in *New York Review of Books*, 21 February 1980, p. 19.

ROSEN, E. (1978), Trans. Copernicus (c. 1530).

ROSENBERG, J.D. (1963), *The Darkening Glass*. London: Routledge and Kegan Paul.

ROSENSHINE, B.V. (1979), 'Content, time and direct instruction' in Peterson, P.L. and Walberg, H.J. *Research on Teaching*. Berkeley, Calif.: McCutchan.

RYLE, G. (1949), *The Concept of Mind*. London: Hutchinson.

—— (1963), 'Ordinary language' in Caton, C. (ed.), *Philosophy and Ordinary Language*. Urbana, Ill.: Illinois University Press. (Orig. publ. in the *Philosophical Review*, 62, 1953, pp. 167–86.)

SACKS, S. (ed.) (1979), *On Metaphor*. Chicago: University of Chicago Press

SARTRE, J.P. (1955), 'François Mauriac and freedom' in *Literary and Philosophical Essays*. New York: Criterion Books.

SCHEFFLER, I. (1960), *The Language of Education*. Springfield Ill.: C.C. Thomas.

SCHIMMEL, A. (1975), *Mystical Dimensions of Islam*. Chapel Hill, N.C.: University of North Carolina Press.

SCHON, D. (1963), *The Displacement of Concepts*. London: Tavistock.

SCOTT, G. (1914, 1980), *The Architecture of Humanism*. London: Architectural Press.

SEARLE, J.R. (1969), *Speech Acts*. Cambridge: The University Press.

SHIBLES, W.A. (1971), *Metaphor: An annotated bibliography and history*. Whitewater, Wisc.: Language Press.

SMITH, G.G. (ed.) (1904), Sir Philip Sidney, *An Apologie for Poetry* (1595) in

Elizabethan Critical Essays, I. Oxford: Clarendon Press.

SOCKETT, H. (1980), *Accountability in the English Educational System.* Sevenoaks: Hodder and Stoughton.

SONTAG, S. (1979), *On Photography.* London: Penguin.

SPEDDING, J., ELLIS R.L. and HEATH, D.D. (eds.) (1857), *The Works of Francis Bacon* III. London: Longman.

SPRATT, T. (1667), *History of the Royal Society.* London: J. Martyn.

STEBBING, L.S. (1942), *A Modern Introduction to Logic.* London: Methuen.

STEINER, G. (1972), 'In a post culture' in *Extra-Territorial.* London: Faber.

STENHOUSE, L. (1975), *An Introduction to Curriculum Research and Development.* London: Heinemann.

STEVENSON, C.L. (1944), *Ethics and Language.* New Haven, Conn.: Yale University Press.

TANNER, J.M. (1978), *Foetus into Man.* London: Basic Books.

TAYLOR, D.M. (1970), *Explanation and Meaning.* Cambridge: The University Press.

TAYLOR, W. (1978), 'Values and accountability' in Becher, T., Maclure, S. (eds.) *Accountability in Education.* Windsor: NFER Publishing.

—— (1980) 'Accountability: concept, movement and metaphor.' Canberra: Proceedings of the 1979 Conference of the Australian Council for Educational Administration

—— (1981), 'Quality control: analysis and comment.' *Educational Administration,* 9(1), pp. 1–20.

THOMSON, J.J. (1907), *The Corpuscular Theory of Matter.* London: Constable.

—— (1936), *Reflections and Recollections.* London: G. Bell and Sons.

TURBAYNE, C.M. (1962), *The Myth of Metaphor.* New Haven, Conn.: Yale University Press.

TYLER, R.W. (1949), *Basic Principles of Curriculum and Instruction.* Chicago: University of Chicago Press

WAISMANN, F. (1965), *The Principles of Linguistic Philosophy* (ed. Harré, R.). London: Macmillan.

WALKERDINE, V. and CORRAN, G. (1981), *The Practice of Reason.* University of London Institute of Education (mimeo).

WALLACE, W. and MILLER, A.V. Trans. of Hegel's *Philosophy of Mind.* London: Oxford University Press.

WEISSKOPF, V.F. (1960), 'The visual appearance of rapidly moving objects.' *Physics Today,* September, pp. 24–7.

WHITEHEAD, A.N. (1929), *Process and Reality.* Cambridge: The University Press.

—— (1948), *Science and the Modern World*. New York: New American Library.

WHITLEY, J.S. (1970), *Golding: Lord of the Flies*. London: Edward Arnold.

WHORF, J.B. (1956), *Language, Thought and Reality*. New York: Wiley.

WILKINS, M. (1966), 'Genetics: are there things we should not know?' *The Sunday Times*, 6 January.

WILLIAMS, G. (1980), *Figures of Thought in Roman Poetry*. New Haven, Conn.: Yale University Press

WILLIAMS, L.P. (1968) (ed.), *Relativity Theory: Its Origins and Impact on Modern Thought*. New York: Wiley.

WISDOM, J. (1952), 'Ludwig Wittgenstein: 1934-37.' *Mind*, 61.

WITTGENSTEIN, L. (1953), *Philosophical Investigations* (trans. G.E.M. Anscombe). Oxford: Basil Blackwell.

WOOD, D. (1981), 'Philosophy and metaphor: the revenge of metaphor.' Unpublished paper read at the City University, 2 March.

WOODWARD, W.H. (1964 edn.), *Erasmus Concerning the Aim and Method of Education*. New York: Teachers College.

YEATS, W.B. (1950), *Collected Poems*. London: Macmillan.

YAGI, E. (1964), '*Nagaoka's Saturnian atomic model, 1903*' *Japanese Studies in the History of Science*, 3, pp. 29-47.

YOUNG, T. (1804), 'Reply to the animadversions of the Edinburgh reviewers' in Peacock, George (ed.) *Miscellaneous Works of Thomas Young*, Vol. 1. London: John Murray.

Index